Contents

Preface

This book might never have existed. Or it might have existed in a different form. I had a mind to write a more scholarly book, dealing with just some of the topics that are addressed here. But I somehow found my way into neighbouring fields, and wrote instead about the environment. And then, teaching philosophy of religion, I thought I saw a gap for a textbook. Again, it's unwritten. The book you're looking at now couples ideas from those different sources, with much about life and death, some about immortality, and a little about the population explosion. The textbook is now dead in the water, while the scholarly book should, in time, take shape.

My interest in these topics goes back a fair way, to my time as a graduate student in Santa Barbara. Tony Brueckner taught there, and some of the things he'd written, with John Fischer, about the badness of death struck me as deeply interesting and profoundly wrong. Around the same time I came across Derek Parfit's *Reasons and Persons*. Without these people, and their writings, my life today would be unaccountably different. I more or less gave up on epistemology, metaphysics and history of philosophy, and focused instead on these questions of life and death.

Several people have read and commented on various chapters, in various of their incarnations. I've gained much from their feedback, and thank them for their interest and their time. These people are Tina Beattie, Ann Gallagher, Steve Holland, Gary Kemp, Carrie Mercier, Catherine Morris, John Shand, Helena Silver, Andrew Ward, and Penelope Whitworth. Many other people have helped in a less direct way, for I've read papers dealing with the themes of several chapters in various places, including the universities of York, Glasgow, Cardiff and the Open University, benefiting always from those audiences' comments.

10 good questions about life and death

christopher belshaw

Blackwell
Publishing

BLACKWELL PUBLISHING

350 Main Street, Malden, MA 02148-5020, USA
9600 Garsington Road, Oxford OX4 2DQ, UK
550 Swanston Street, Carlton, Victoria 3053, Australia

First published 2005 by Blackwell Publishing Ltd

1   2005

Library of Congress Cataloging-in-Publication Data

Belshaw, Christopher.
10 good questions about life and death / Christopher Belshaw.
p.   cm.
Includes bibliographical references and index.
ISBN 1-4051-2577-2 (hardcover : alk. paper) – ISBN 1-4051-2604-3
(pbk. : alk. paper)
1. Life.   2. Values.   I. Title: Ten good questions about
life and death.   II. Title.

BD431.B387 2005
128—dc22

2004021396

ISBN-13: 978-1-4051-2577-2 (hardcover : alk. paper) –
ISBN-13: 978-1-4051-2604-5 (pbk. : alk. paper)

A catalogue record for this title is available from the British Library.

Set in 11.5/13pt Perpetua
by Graphicraft Limited, Hong Kong
Printed and bound in the United Kingdom
by TJ International, Padstow, Cornwall

The publisher's policy is to use permanent paper from mills that operate a sustainable forestry policy, and which has been manufactured from pulp processed using acid-free and elementary chlorine-free practices. Furthermore, the publisher ensures that the text paper and cover board used have met acceptable environmental accreditation standards.

For further information on
Blackwell Publishing, visit our website:
www.blackwellpublishing.com

'This fine book explores these most inescapable of questions with a concern for what can honestly and reasonably be believed. It is free of any untoward ambition to announce surprising discoveries, but neither is it anxious to reinforce easy pieties. The reader may be distressed that so many religious or metaphysical profundities turn out to be houses of cards, but also reassured that they are not needed in order to think clearly and usefully about life and death.'

Gary Kemp, University of Glasgow

'This is a witty and engaging discussion of the main issues that arise when we ask searching questions about the human condition, especially about our mortality and the meaning of our lives. It invites us to relish the deep questions rather than find shallow answers, and even when I disagreed with the direction the analysis takes (as the author cheerfully invites the reader to do), I was glad for the intellectual stimulation provided by this sharp-minded inquiry, which is often both playful and profound, and always clear and interesting. It is notable for making many important distinctions and for giving numerous illustrations, including real-life examples that are absorbing and appropriate, as well as hypothetical mental experiments that are sometimes fanciful, but invariably clever and insightful. Use it as a friendly and smart coach who can help students wrestle with high thoughts about the big questions while keeping their feet on the ground.'

Edward Langerak, St. Olaf College

'In this very engaging book Belshaw addresses questions that really are good ones – the deep questions of our existence that have troubled thinking people everywhere. Philosophers should have something to say about these issues, and Belshaw tackles them in a way that manages to be both erudite and entertaining. This book is a must for all reflective people – philosophers and lay thinkers alike – whose minds naturally turn to questions of life and death.'

Stephen Holland, University of York

'This is a very engaging, highly readable introduction to some of the great questions of life and death. Belshaw is a thoughtful and skilled philosopher who writes in a crisp and lively way. Allow me to add one more question: What's not to like?'

John Fischer, University of California, Riverside

Our birth is nothing but our death begun
(Edward Young, *Night Thoughts*)

I also need to give special thanks to Tom Baldwin, for inviting me to teach courses at the University of York that have fed directly into this book, and thanks as well to the students there, stimulating in several ways, and encounters with whom can make one glad to be alive.

Chapter One

Where Can I Find Answers?

Just before she died she asked, 'What is the answer?' No answer came. She laughed and said, 'In that case, what is the question?' Then she died.
(The last words of Gertrude Stein)

In the middle of nowhere two men, looking like tramps, are waiting for something to happen. They need to make sense of their lives. It isn't easy. One of them considers suicide, but then thinks better of it. The other sums up their lot – a painful birth, a painful death, with little of consequence in between. They're half-expecting someone. If he comes – if he exists – he might put things into place, give their lives some shape. Another man does come along with a boy. They stay a while, then they leave. Later they return, and then leave again. But he wasn't the one they half-expected. And, this apart, nothing happens.

These characters in *Waiting for Godot* reveal familiar concerns. What matters? How are we to live our lives? What are we to hope for? Can God and religion help? Is it bad that it will end? Many of us share these concerns, and, even if not relentlessly, ask ourselves such questions. And just such questions are asked in this book. They can seem straightforward. Yet they're not at all easy to answer. Beckett's characters get nowhere with them, and nor, for much of the time, do we. Why is this? It's going to be useful to think more about the sorts of questions asked here, see what makes them difficult, and consider what, if anything, holds them together.

They share a common theme. They're all, and obviously, questions about life and death. And, both for Beckett in his plays, and for me in the chapters that follow, they are about human life and human death. They deal with the basics of our existence, the span of our days and what, if anything, lies beyond. It's not surprising, then, that these are questions that concern us all.

And then they share an approach to that theme. They're all philosophical questions. That, too, might be obvious, either from where you found the book, or from skimming through it, or from looking at the cover. Even so, it might not be obvious what philosophy is. How does it connect with the apparently straightforward questions here? And what sorts of answers, if any, can it hope to offer?

Philosophy

But we can start with what it isn't. Philosophy isn't a science. It doesn't ask a lot of difficult factual questions, ones that need laboratories, big grants, teams of researchers to answer them. And because it doesn't ask such questions, doesn't in this way depend on and go after the facts, philosophy is unlike classics, black studies, law, and a host of further subjects besides. Like science, these also require a lot of real-world information, poking around in libraries and archives, devising experiments, surveys, and questionnaires. Of course, there are, as well, many scientific and quasi-scientific questions about life and death. It isn't just the topics that put us in the business of philosophy. So we might ask, for example, how does a living thing develop? How many died during the 1665 plague? What's the Buddhist angle on the sanctity of life? And what do Americans believe about heaven? These questions, all factual, are different in kind from the ones asked here.

There's another thing that philosophy isn't. It isn't narrow, unified, easily categorized. Its reputation is better than it was, but a lot of people still think of it as abstruse and high-flown – given to questions that have little or no bearing on everyday life: What is truth? Are we all dreaming? How is mathematics possible? Certainly, large parts of philosophy are like this, and anyone looking at a shelf in a university bookshop or at the contents pages of most academic journals will find much that's baffling, technical and inbred. A lot of philosophy does indeed deal with questions of metaphysics, and the fundamental nature of reality, and a lot more is centred on epistemology, and with what we can know of things, fundamental or not. Even so, there's a good deal that has a more straightforward connection with our lives, and tackles important and familiar issues of everyday concern. So questions about the rights and wrongs of abortion, war, or capital punishment, about whether we ought to give aid to the victims of famine and drought, whether the environment, or art, matters beyond its usefulness to us, whether animals have rights, all figure in an increasing number of philosophy books and courses. There's the surprisingly long-running radio programme, *The Moral Maze*, which picks up on some dilemma of the week, and then subjects its victims to a barrage of questions about where they stand on the matter. There are columns in newspapers, subplots in novels and films, topics in a range of school exams. And there are discussions of such issues in cafés and bars everywhere. So it has its theoretical and practical sides, its history and its present, its scholars and its practitioners. It shouldn't be surprising that it's in this way wide-ranging. Just as there's a lot of variety in science, and literature, and art, so too for philosophy.

And it isn't narrow, isn't unified, in a further way. Even while agreeing that it's not a science, people nevertheless disagree about how best to approach it. Look for philosophy in a bookshop or on the internet and you'll find, as well as works by Plato, Kant and Wittgenstein, material connected with mysticism, Eastern religion, crystals, and lifestyle issues. Some people think of philosophy as involving trances, mantras, drugs and still other ways to attain a higher reality, a state where all is one. Others, in contrast, see it as hung up on reason, logic and analysis, quibbling about the meaning of words, insisting that we always first define our terms. Both approaches are at, or near to the extremes. Even so, what connects them, and connects them as well with the middle ground, is the idea that philosophy has a lot to do with understanding, and perhaps even benefiting from understanding, some difficult topics. There might be disagreement about how this understanding is to be achieved, but certainly it's this, or wisdom, clarity, or enlightenment that is, as ever, at philosophy's core.

About This Book

Though philosophy is a big subject, with many different parts, its scale is not reflected in this book. And though it can be tackled in a number of different ways, there is little of that variety here. There is just the one set of questions – some basic issues about life and death. And there is just one approach taken to answering them – reason and argument. But I'll say some more about both these points.

First, the range. I mentioned some of the more familiar philosophical questions above. But besides those questions – about abortion, punishment, rights, and so on – there are others, more fundamental, about what matters to us, what's of value. And it's on the basis of answers to, and beliefs about, these further questions that many of our judgements regarding morality are based. Yet while the moral questions are often openly debated, these underlying beliefs tend to be taken for granted. Just two examples. We can spend a lot of time arguing about the rights and wrongs of capital punishment. But it's typically going to be assumed throughout that it's a good thing to live, and a bad thing to die. It's largely because of these beliefs that taking someone's life seems such a big issue. Or we wonder how God, if there is a God, could justify a system in which some of us suffer eternal damnation, while others enjoy paradise forever. And the assumption, often, is that whether or not it actually exists, heaven would surely be a good thing. Believe that, and getting there becomes important. So in both these cases the questions about morality – about what we should do to each other, or about what God should do to us – rest upon these underlying beliefs, first, about the value of life, second about the value of heaven. And in both cases the moral debate might well take a different turn once these underlying value assumptions begin to be explored.

Many of the questions in this book deal with these matters of value. Those that don't are closely connected with such matters. So rather than rehearse the relatively familiar questions about morality – and there are lots of books that do just this – I'm looking here at what lies beneath. And if questions of morality are important, then these underpinning questions are more important still. What I want to do, then, is focus on just a small number of issues that concern us all, and that in one way or another, acknowledged or not, help shape almost everything we do. The questions here come from different directions – from religion, medicine, population theory, puzzles about identity – but they all point to just a pair of closely connected themes – the good life, and the good life for me. Closely connected obviously, but nevertheless distinct. For not only do I want to know what makes a life worth living, gives it meaning and significance, I want to know as well whether this worthwhile life is one that I should care about, whether it will in fact be a life that I might hope to live.

Second, the approach. You shouldn't get the wrong idea about how pure it is. I don't want to promote the caricature of the philosopher as some kind of ivory-towered, egg-headed calculating machine, a tweedy version of Mr Spock. The emphasis is on reason, but not to the exclusion of all else. And though there's an abiding concern to make things clear, there's no corresponding concern to pepper the whole thing with definitions, dotting all the 'i's', crossing every 't'. For if the question isn't overly technical, nor, I think, should be the approach to answering it. And with questions about life, death and meaning, attempts at too much precision can only mislead. There's a related point here. Given such questions, then facts about our lives, and our views and beliefs about them, are needed for answers. This is another reason the ivory tower philosopher can't get things right. Why? Because to answer these questions you do need some understanding of human nature, some grasp of what makes us tick. One way to acquire such understanding is to think about your own life, and the lives of people you know. Another is find out something of just how people have ticked in the past, and elsewhere, either by looking at history, or at biography, or at novels, plays, poems and films. Don't think I'm going back on an earlier point. I'm not now saying that we need to dig about, collect lots of facts. It's often little more than a fairly basic knowledge, a general understanding, that is needed here. And such knowledge can be picked up or borrowed from elsewhere, with the philosopher relying on others to provide the right sort of information, rather than investigating these matters afresh.

I can say something else about this book. I ask the questions. I do some philosophy. And then I offer some answers. Yet there'll be people who are suspicious about this entire procedure. Factual questions have answers. Others don't. That's one suspicion. It all sounds preachy and dogmatic. That's another. Are these suspicions well founded? Hardly surprising, but I don't think so.

A Case Study

He spends most of his time in the market place, in Athens, trying to draw people into conversation. Not just anybody – bigwigs, generals, politicians, aristocrats, so-called philosophers, and young men who think of themselves as the bigwigs of the future. And not just any conversation – Socrates is concerned, much as I am here, first with questions of value, with what makes life worth living, and, second with questions about these questions – what are they like?, why are they tricky?, where are the answers? His tactic, usually, is to feign ignorance, catch his targets off guard, flatter them, and then get them to make fools of themselves. They hate him for it. And in the end it costs him his life.

Why, though, bother with these conversations? Why make all this fuss? There are two views that Socrates opposes, and that he wants to show are wrong. First, there's the view that just because of their status, these people have any special authority in these matters. It's one thing to think a general can successfully command an army in the field, or that a lawyer can get his client off some embezzlement charge, and another to suppose that either has any particular weight in the wider moral and value questions. Second, there's the view, seemingly at odds with the first, that there are just no experts, no authorities, in such matters, and that everyone's opinion is as good as the next person's. Think this, and you'll probably think that whenever disputes of this sort arise, the best and fairest way to resolve them is simply to put things to a vote. There might seem to be real difficulties in threading a way through these positions – rejecting both traditional authority, on the one hand, and a free-for-all populism, on the other – but Socrates manages it. He keeps on insisting that just as there's a need for experts in, say, pot-making, horse-training, or flute-playing, so too there's a similar need where the good life is concerned. It's important to have well-made pots about the house, and so it's important to seek out a proven expert before you buy. It's even more important to make a good job of living your life, and so even more important to get the best advice about how to do this, neither swallowing mere claptrap, nor blundering along on your own.

But then what's wrong with generals, lawyers and politicians? Why can't we learn from them? Well, it's just that once they're off their own patch, they rarely know what they're talking about. And this is where it matters that Socrates, like many of us today, lives in a kind of democracy, a society where it's always possible, in principle at least, to challenge authority, insist it explains itself. There's a disinclination, then as now, to show someone unqualified and unconditional respect, or to sit, obedient and uncomplaining, at the feet of a guru or master. And Socrates is particularly good at this kind of challenge, at taking the wind from the sails of these self-appointed experts, and proving, usually in front of a crowd of amused onlookers, that their so-called expertise is nothing more than a sham. Yet there's always a problem within a more open society, one that encourages supposedly healthy debate – it can be tempting, having knocked people off their pedestals, simply then to walk away, leaving a mess behind. And many of his contemporaries thought of Socrates as a merely destructive force, unpicking at their society's still delicate fabric with no thought of tomorrow. They had him wrong. Socrates cared about Athens, its citizens, and their somewhat fragile and un-settled state. He wanted to help put things right, to persuade people to think hard about the most basic issues facing them, and to find genuine experts in the art of living well. It wasn't going to be easy. Where to look? He gives no straight answer to this question, nor does he offer himself as the fount of all wisdom. But what he does do is insist on a test for expertise. And it's reason. If someone's claims don't stand up to reason, if they don't square with each other, and with other things they say they know, if they're at odds with things beyond all reasonable doubt, then those claims can hardly be accepted. There is no blind authority. But there is authority nevertheless, derived from reason, from making sense, from withstanding criticism and robust questioning. Find the experts. Listen to what they have to say. But then their answers are going to stand or fall, in the end, on their own terms.

Experts and Expertise

On this point little has changed. And those suspicions still survive today. We think that either these questions can't really be answered, and all we can do is note different responses to them, with one person's opinion counting as much as the next. Or if there are answers, then they must be difficult to provide, depending on specialist knowledge and expertise, with everyday beliefs, and everyday objections, counting for little or nothing. So it's either anything goes, or there are authorities, and it's a kind of science, after all.

But now what's fallen between two stools here is the idea of a middle position, the idea that there's genuine progress to be made, genuinely better and worse views to be had, and yet that we're all able to contribute to this progress, and help distinguish between these views. Take just one question: should euthanasia be permitted? We don't have to think that there's no real point in asking this, and that one opinion is just as good as the next. Nor need we suppose that doctors, or lawyers, must know what's best here. We can have an intelligent debate, consider the pros and cons, chew things over, and come, in the end, to a well-supported view. Or another: should Muslims, or Catholics, or Jews, have their own schools? Again there are serious moral issues here, and though historians, educationalists, clerics will all have a big input the answer won't derive simply from their views alone. It's a matter of concern, and importance for us all.

So, is there philosophical expertise or not? Yes, but it's of a somewhat peculiar kind. Take history, medicine, geography. For most of us, and for most of the time, there's little option but to take what is said here on trust, believe in the specialists, accept their word. There are just too many facts. And there is, in such areas, a fairly standard and familiar notion of expertise, knowledge-based, cumulative, and not readily open to outside appraisal. But now contrast this with, say, a grand master in chess. He's an expert in a different sense – it isn't that he knows a lot more about chess than the rest of us but rather that, partly through innate talent, and partly through hard work, he's just better at it. Even so, you can understand what he's doing, follow the moves, see how good he is. You don't have to take anything on trust. It's similar with maths – I read only today in the newspaper of a top mathematician who describes his job, not as collecting more information, but as taking the relatively little he has, and then sitting and thinking about it. And it's similar again, elsewhere, with tennis players, jazz pianists, actors. Their talent depends on skill and understanding, rather than knowledge. And it's transparent. We can see what they're up to, judge for ourselves how good they are, and rank them one against the other.

It's the same, more or less, with philosophers. They mix a taste for certain questions – often abstract, general, long-standing – with a range of skills – putting things clearly, analysing and constructing arguments, sticking with a relatively small point. But there isn't a vast fund of knowledge that the philosopher needs to draw on. And I say the same, more or less, because philosophical expertise isn't transparent in a way strictly analogous to tennis or chess. Sad but true, we're not all as reasonable as each other. And so we're not all equally able to assess the merits of some philosophical argument.

Who Needs Philosophy?

Yet even if there are things to think about, and questions to answer, is it really clear that we need philosophy in order to go about this? Think of other things – religion, schools, novels and plays, stories of great lives, even the influence of your own family. Don't we already find plenty there that deals with the art of living well? Why look further?

There's something to the point here, and no one's going to suggest that the questions in this book are the province of philosophy alone. Didn't I start, after all, with the gist of a well-known play? But it's one thing to raise questions, and another to provide answers. And it's often true that when answers come directly from these others sources, then they're less solid, less accurate, and less convincing than those that philosophy might provide. This isn't always a problem – the best thing with children, often, is just to tell them what's right and wrong, what matters and what doesn't, rather than to reason with them, and talk everything through. And on the larger scale, Kant thought that for societies, too, there are periods when instruction is better than debate. But for us actively to take part in discussion of these issues is, individually and collectively, a better thing, and a symptom of greater maturity, than unquestioningly following the dictates of others. Even then there's perhaps no distinctive need for philosophy. For while some religions lay down the law, and insist on blind faith, others ask for reflection and criticism, and stress the guiding power of conscience. And while some novels, some films, sweep you along, breathless, on a tide of emotion, others encourage a certain distancing from character and plot, inviting you instead to think through the issues they raise. In schools and in homes there's a similar contrast, often related to age, with passive obedience giving way to more active and even-handed involvement in the matters to hand.

Yet in all these cases, rather than thinking it redundant, it's perhaps better to suppose that some proto-philosophical activity is already taking place. And surely this is right. For there isn't, of course, philosophy on the one hand, and the rest of culture on the other. There is, instead, a seamlessness, and differences of emphasis, with identifiable philosophical approaches and concerns emerging, by degrees, from a range of more familiar debates.

There's a bearing in all this on the claim, often made, that we're all philosophers. Is this true? On the one hand I've suggested that maybe we can all engage with some philosophical issue, while on the other I've allowed that some of us might be better at this than others. So, are we all philosophers, or is there just a happy few?

Well, almost everyone asks themselves, at some time or other, certain philosophical questions – can terrorism ever be justified? Is there a God? Might it all be a dream? We ask these questions as children, when we're drunk and maudlin, in response to events reported in the news. Of course, some of us ask such questions more often than others, but there's hardly anyone who shows no interest whatsoever. And then, inevitably, almost everyone tries to provide these questions with answers. Again, either because of some innate ability, or because of their training, or both, some spend longer, and are better at it than others. Even so, the differences between, first, good and bad philosophers and, second, philosophers and non-philosophers are in the end matters of degree, rather than of kind. It's the same with football, or music. Gordon can kick a ball around, run up and down the left wing, and if he's playing with friends from work can even score the odd goal, but he's no Ronaldino. Is he a footballer? He says he is, and shows you his fancy footwork. Carrie plays piano and bass guitar, neither particularly well, but she's got a good sense of rhythm and knows when the singer's out of tune. Is she a musician? She denies it, pointing to her limited abilities, and the fact that she's passed no exams. And yet in both cases it's surely a waste of time to fuss about these labels. We might well know just how good a player he is, how useful she is in a band, without deciding whether some particular cap fits. So, similarly, we might say that, in one sense, everyone's a philosopher. But there are substantial differences in ability. And if someone wants to restrict the term to those who are good at it, or professionals, it won't much matter.

The Answers

So where are they? I've probably said enough already to make this clear. There are answers, of sorts, in the book itself. Each chapter, this included, sets out to address and reply to the question of its title. The answers are not always complete and might not always be satisfying. But they are as complete and as satisfying as I can, in this space, make them. So what I've tried to do is to put things clearly, presenting both what I think is the right view on the different topics – insisting, for example, that death is often bad, that there's no good reason to believe in an afterlife, that it needn't matter if the best people aren't born – and at the same time giving arguments in favour of that view, and reasons for supposing that it's right. And this is what the book is about – asking these philosophical questions about life and death, pulling the questions apart, moving towards answers, giving those answers their proper support. There are other things as well. I sometimes point out where a particular idea originated, or give the names of people who have held, or objected to, a certain view. And I sometimes refer to, and sometimes invent stories that illustrate a particular point, either to make it clearer or to show how philosophy is continuous with everyday concerns. But the emphasis throughout is on the questions and their answers, and most of such comment, such citing of facts, is peripheral.

It's important to notice, though, that the answers given here are in two senses less than authoritative. First, many philosophers will disagree with them. So people who've spent at least as long as I have in thinking and reading about these issues, people who've taught more courses, read more books, and who are all round at least as able, will have different views, and be convinced that contrary answers are easily as good as those offered here. Think about how respectable scientists still argue about the big bang, or how historians are at loggerheads over the causes of the French Revolution. Second, and in contrast to these examples, I don't want to pull rank over any careful reader. You will agree with my answers, if you do, not because you take them on trust, but because, having thought things through, you are persuaded by the arguments. Mistakes – even if you think you couldn't have done better yourself – are going to be visible; like breaking the rules in chess, or over-hitting the top spin in tennis. For in an important sense, the authority for answers to such questions lies within each of us, and not somewhere beyond. Even so, it's hard, usually, to get very far on your own. And in a further important sense, what happens here is always a collaboration, with answers coming from a team – I make suggestions, you think about them, and form your own view.

Matters of Style

I might have adopted a different approach. Some writers would have tried to be even-handed, giving the best arguments on each side, balancing the pros against the cons, and leaving their own position, their own views, well hidden. And they might have thought that if the point is to encourage people to make up their own minds, to leave them free to decide, then that is the way to go. For surely it's inevitable that we are influenced by what we read, and so if some philosopher is free to present his own point of view with no contrary position rearing its head, then, many people, especially those relatively new to the subject, are going to be swayed by this. So if I'm honest in saying that I want you to come to a view of your own, then I would have adopted this dispassionate, stand-back, approach.

But it's worth being clear about this. For it's easy to run two things together – giving the best arguments on both sides, and being even-handed, balanced, uncommitted. Sometimes the truth is hard to discover, and then contrary arguments may well carry equal weight. But at other times there's pretty much an open and shut case, with the best arguments on one side clearly trouncing their rivals. It's hard to see, for example, how there could be worthwhile cases both for and against racism, or torturing animals, or for believing in fairies. And it's hard to see here how a fence-sitting book, giving its readers supposedly balanced argu-ments, could be altogether honest. It might also be annoying. Ages back, the Greek philosopher Carneades was invited to Rome to show off his talents. The first day he argued, convincingly, that justice, at bottom, is altogether natural. The next day he was equally convincing in arguing that it's entirely a matter of convention. The Romans didn't know where they were, only that at least once they'd been conned, and Carneades had to leave town. So much for balance.

This still leaves, however, the further option: give the best arguments, however strong, and then step back and allow them to speak for themselves. Might that be preferred? It might, but I don't try to do that here. This isn't a textbook, and I'm not trying to be a teacher. I'm trying to answer the questions. So although I give objections to the views put forward, I make it clear that, at least in many cases, I think those objections can be defeated. And I find it neither easy nor interesting to avoid taking sides.

That's one point about style. There's another that needs to be mentioned. I'll be honest, this isn't the most exciting book you'll ever read. It might not even be the most exciting philosophy book. But if so, that's in part because, once again, I'm simply trying to answer the questions. But I should explain something.

There are two contrasting styles in philosophy – on the one hand are the system builders, intent, often, on a philosophy of everything, with the different parts fitting well together, and on the other are the sceptics and critics, much given to deconstructing, and finding fault with what the system builders think they've achieved. Often, of course, the system builders write the longer books. Go back to near the beginning, and there's the stark contrast between Socrates and Plato, with the earlier philosopher's unscripted conversations set against the latter's many tomes. And while Socrates was primarily a questioner, claiming, even if not always convincingly, to know nothing, Plato, at least for periods in his life, produced a coherent and well-structured whole. A similar contrast occurs in the eighteenth century, between the Scottish philosopher David Hume, and, in Germany, Immanuel Kant. Hume sets out his stall as a self-confessed sceptic, concerned, above all else, to show that the systems of his contemporaries and predecessors, though they promise much, invariably fail to deliver. They're impressive, elaborate and showy, but ambition gets the better of them, and they're too easily undermined. And it was precisely Hume's sceptical work that motivated Kant to develop, toward the end of his life, his three big books, once more putting an ambitious and systematic philosophy firmly on the map. The contrast surfaces again in the following century. Though they're often linked together, Schopenhauer's philosophy of pessimism, erected on Kantian foundations, is an altogether larger and more structured work than the improvisatory, allusive and often inconsistent writings of Nietzsche. And Wittgenstein covered the angles here, first building a system but then later, after something of a holiday, knocking it down. I'm on the sceptical side. It isn't merely temperament, although that must be a part of it. More important, it seems to me that when it aims high, philosophy typically overreaches itself. Life is messy, as too is what we say and think about it, and systematic philosophy, looking for clean lines, elegance, precision, seems to do too little justice to this. It's more or less the same whenever theorizing about human activity gets carried away with itself – communism, monetarism and faddy diets are all less able to respond to the complexity of our interests and needs than more pragmatic and open-ended solutions. If you want to lose weight, eat less. And if you want a better life, think more. That's the gist of it. This doesn't, though, leave the more sceptical philosophy with nothing to do. It can puncture the pretensions of its overblown and high-flown rivals, on the one hand. And (not entirely separately) it can function as a corrective to everyday errors and confusions, on the other. And that's quite a lot. The upshot, then, is that many of the arguments given in this book are in important ways critical. I often find fault with more spectacular and heady views. And I suggest, often, that a murkier position is better. Further, in many cases the answers I favour are closer to common sense, and thus are already familiar, and for that reason are less exciting than some of their competitors. I don't want to overdo this, and don't want to deny that there are (at least as I believe) in every chapter both ideas and arguments which many people are likely to find provocative and novel. But they are the exception; and sensible, moderate and, I hope, reassuring views prevail. So, for example, I suggest that some lives are more meaningful than others, rather than that they are all irredeemably absurd. Similarly, I argue that it's often but not invariably bad to die, and thus reject the views both that death is always bad, and that it's never bad. And already in this chapter I've wanted to say that we can well enough understand the claim that everyone's a philosopher, without getting too steamed upon about whether or not we agree. None of this is particularly surprising or challenging. But it's all, I think, true. And it's truth I'm after.

I'll make one more point here, Someone once said that I seemed myself not to be particularly excited or gripped by the issues I'm trying here to deal with. There might be something in this. Anyone brought up in 1950s' Yorkshire, rugby and coal mines to the west, fenland to the east, bubble and squeak for tea, learns soon enough to keep excitement and enthusiasm under wraps. It's the northern variant of the stiff upper lip. But if I didn't care, and deeply, about these questions, and their answers, I wouldn't have written this book.

Chapter Two

Is Life Sacred?

I call upon all Americans to reflect upon the sanctity of human life. Let us recognize the day with appropriate ceremonies in our homes and places of worship, rededicate ourselves to compassionate service on behalf of the weak and defenseless, and reaffirm our commitment to respect the life and dignity of every human being.

(George W. Bush, proclaiming Sunday, 20 January 2002, as National Sanctity of Human Life Day)

I'm listening to an afternoon programme on the radio. One woman is trying to keep two more from tearing each other apart. The first of these women, a professor so and so, from such and such university, is vehemently opposed to euthanasia, and insists we should all go on living, and should be glad to go on living, until the more or less natural end. The other is someone who works closely with people who are terminally ill, some of whom want to die, and she's incensed that this other woman should think she knows what's best for them. They're arguing about the sanctity of life.

Issues like this get under the skin. And often, when people are for or against this sanctity view, they're eager to put their ideas into practice, to get people to act in certain ways, and not in others, to change or to defend the laws of the land, to fight more strongly for life, or to be more accepting of death. Passions are roused. And because so much hangs on it, it seems important to find out as soon as possible where the truth lies, and which of these people are right, and which are wrong.

Yet before trying to decide whether life is sacred or not, it's a good idea, if we can, to sort out just what it is that people believe when they believe, or say they believe, in the sanctity of life. For it can be much less clear than it seems at first. Often people assume they know what an opponent thinks, before they've really worked out exactly what their position is. And sometimes people haven't really thought through what they themselves mean, when they talk about the sanctity of life. So the first thing here is to try to sift through the different kinds of things that might be meant in claiming that life is sacred. There's big spread of positions, and some of them might seem to be obviously non-starters. Then it'll be worth focusing on a couple of more plausible and at the same time more popular views, and looking at them in a bit more detail, to see what they're about. And if we can be clearer about what they say, we can go on to the big question – are these views true?

Lives

There's a complication, first, about life. Some people, in claiming that life is sacred, are thinking only about human beings, and human life. And a lot of the time that you hear about the issue on the radio or television, or read about it in the papers, or find that it's being talked about in parliament, or the courts, it's human life – and perhaps especially issues to do with abortion, and euthanasia, and maybe also capital punishment – that they're concerned with. Others, though, think that animal life, or at least some animal life, is sacred as well. So while some vegetarians avoid meat on health grounds, others think that cows, rabbits, turkeys, and maybe also salmon and oysters should be free to live out their lives, just as we, usually, can live out ours. Mary Wollstonecraft seems to have thought this, in her stories designed for the moral education of children, and it's not much later in the nineteenth century that the RSPCA was founded to look after the interests of animals. A little later still, the last straw for Nietzsche, before his descent into madness, was to come across a man whipping and beating his horse in the streets of Turin. Still others believe that all life is sacred – humans, animals, and plants as well. Although he talked most often about the need for us to have reverence for life, the musician, doctor, and philosopher Albert Schweitzer seems to have been one of the best-known proponents of this wider sanctity view, and some people think that Prince Charles has a similar stance. And a lot of environmentalists, especially the self-styled deep ecologists, objecting to motorways, bypasses, airport runways, believe that all life is of value.

Attitudes

There's a second issue, more complex, about our attitude to the lives we think of as sacred. Again, there are narrower and wider views. Some people insist that it's wrong for us to kill, even though they're not always troubled by deaths that can be put down to natural causes. But more often there's a connection made here, with people opposing killing because they think death is always bad. And then a wider view seems to follow through on what is apparently implied by this, and suggests that we should aim as well to preserve or extend life. So doctors should do what they can to keep their patients alive, rather than, as often happens, allowing them in some circumstances to die. A still wider view is that we shouldn't prevent, or stand in the way of, the creation of life. Catholics, famously, are supposed to believe that contraception is wrong, and that when life is this close, it should not be thwarted. Finally, some people believe life is valuable or sacred in such a way that the more lives there are, the better it is. Not only should we be prepared for babies, if we're bent on sex, but we should be actively looking for people to have sex with, in order that more babies can be born. And, even though things soon go horribly wrong, Dr. Frankenstein seems to have some such view about the value of life when, by artificial means, he sets about creating what turns out to be his monster. This story still resonates with our fears about the abuse of technology, about hubris, but even if we are wary about ourselves making new people, many of us think it would be good if God had created extra planets, with extra lives upon them.

Conditions

When these different positions, first, on the kinds of lives, and, second, on the attitudes to life intersect, then a whole range of possible views emerge. Some of these will appear plausible – if you think life shouldn't be prevented, you'll think it wrong to neuter the cat, and if you think life should be promoted, you'll be among those who planted a millennium tree. Yet others might seem just too extreme and far-fetched to count as serious candidates for the sanctity of life view. Surely no one will think the world ought to contain as many slugs as possible. And no one will think we should do all we can to prevent the death of a nettle. But now there are complications that need to be introduced, which show how these absurd views can be avoided. That there might be some such complications is most obvious, perhaps, in cases of killing.

Think just about human beings. Some people believe that killing human beings is wrong under all conditions, no matter what. But others hold that although killing is wrong in general, there can be exceptions. They might think, for example, that even though life is sacred, capital punishment can be justified. What is wrong is killing the innocent, and it's because some people do exactly this that they can, or should, be killed in turn. In a related manner, some believers in the sanctity of life allow killing in self-defence. Or, again related, they will permit the killing of one to save many. Or the killing of a foetus to save the life of the mother. What these various qualifications suggest is that the restriction on killing is not, for these people, inflexible, but might in some circumstances be lifted. But now this distinction between absolute and conditional views does not concern killing alone, but can surface elsewhere. So, while it's possible to understand the sanctity of life as implying we should promote as many new lives as we can, no matter what, it is also possible, and surely more reasonable, to think that any such injunction must be conditional – start new lives as long as there's space, or if you've got the time, or if they won't interfere with existing lives, or some such condition.

This is an important complication to be clear about. The narrower the view about sanctity, the easier it is to deal in absolutes. The wider the view, the more important it will be, if things aren't going to be hopeless from the start, that other considerations are allowed into the picture. So it really is possible to believe, for example, that killing human beings is always and absolutely wrong, wrong in all circumstances, wrong no matter what. But it's much harder to believe this about killing in general. Take Albert Schweitzer. His view wasn't preposterous. Even though he thought that all life was sacred, and not to be ended without good reason, he still thought we could justifiably kill plants to feed cattle, and then in turn kill cattle to feed human beings.

Values

There's one further complication that needs to be mentioned just here. It's about the kind of value that life has. And it involves making two distinctions, one fairly straightforward, the other a bit trickier.

First, there's a distinction that all sanctity views make. For if you think that life, or maybe just human life, is sacred, you think it has a value or importance beyond its usefulness to others. Life isn't valuable just as a resource or also as means to an end. Even if people, animals and plants have *instrumental* value – postmen deliver mail, hounds sniff out drugs, potatoes help keep us alive – they have, for sanctity believers, another value, and often a more important value, as well. But what sort of value is that? A lot of people want to insist that life, or human life, has *intrinsic* value, or is valuable just in itself. They think life is a good thing independently of its effects or usefulness elsewhere.

But now the harder distinction is this. As well as intrinsic value, there's maybe a space here for talking about *personal* value, as offering another contrast with value of the merely instrumental kind. So as well as thinking that life may be valuable just in itself, we might think it's of value to the person, or maybe even the thing, whose life it is. An example will help:

> *Uncle Joe*. He's old, he's ill, and he's in hospital. Everyone agrees that it's just a matter of time. Katarina, who's always been hard-hearted, thinks it would be better if things could be brought to an end right now. After all, life's no fun for Joe, he can't work, he's no use to anyone, and think of the hospital bills they'd save. Piet's not interested in the money. And he thinks they should do everything possible to manage the pain, make Joe's remaining time a thing of dignity and value, and give him a little more of a life he'd want to live. Vincent agrees about the money, but he's sceptical about whether much more can be done to help Joe. Yet he's opposed to euthanasia, whether or not this is what Joe wants. He thinks that, however bad it is, life should be lived to the end.

Piet and Vincent are both opposed to Katarina's narrow and instrumental slant on human life. But while Piet thinks that Joe's life can be good for him, Vincent seems to believe it's just good in itself, even if it's not good for Joe, that his life should continue, at least until it comes to its natural end.

This idea of personal value is reasonably familiar. Most people, when they are interested in football, or ballet, or whisky, or video games, value these things not because they're useful, or a means to getting something else. They value them just for what they are. But hardly anyone thinks that whisky, for example, is intrinsically valuable, valuable just in itself. Rather, it's valuable only because people actually like it. And the point I want to stress here is that, in contrast to whisky, life might be valuable in either of these ways. It might be good that your life continues only so long as there's something in it for you, only so long as it is of personal value. But life might also be intrinsically valuable, and its continuing good just in itself, independently of whether it's good for you.

Religion, Reason, and a Pair of Views

What exactly does it mean, then, to say that life is sacred? All we've done so far is point to quite a few, maybe too many, things that it could mean, without suggesting any way to choose between them. But perhaps there is a way. For some people think that what we need to do is take the phrase 'the sanctity of life' literally, look carefully at its historical origins, and then its true meaning will come to the surface, with others falling by the way. And taken literally, and looking at its origins, it's clear that there is a connection between ideas of sanctity, and beliefs in religion. More specifically, some people will want to say that this is an essentially Christian notion, and one that is fairly obviously restricted to killing human beings.

Is this right? Not altogether, I think, even though there's quite a bit in it. The idea of sacredness is, at bottom, an idea that sits at the heart of a lot of religion, with its insistence on the holy, on places and things that have been sanctified – groves, icons, temples, bones – and its emphasis on ritual and sacrament. And certainly Christianity is greatly concerned with all this. Certainly too, Christianity, and the Judaism that lies behind it, are greatly concerned with the value of human life in particular – even though the 6th Commandment says, seemingly generally, 'Thou shalt not kill', it's pretty clearly concerned just with human beings. But there's little point in pretending things are altogether black and white here. Maybe even Christianity is concerned with non-human life as well. Some parts of Genesis hint at this, and St. Francis of Assisi certainly thought it should be. And maybe also it's concerned with more than stopping us from killing – one of the things the bible tells us to do is to go forth and multiply, and, as I've noted, many Christians are opposed to contraception. Another thing to notice is that even if ideas about sanctity are central to Christianity, the Bible never expressly say that life is sacred, and neither the Bible in particular nor the Christian tradition in general expressly condemns abortion, or capital punishment, or war. So there's quite a bit of interpretation needed to take some of even the most basic ideas about the sanctity of life out of their Christian setting.

Conversely, there's quite a bit of work needed to keep such ideas out of other religions. Judaism and Islam also put an emphasis, even if not exactly the same emphasis, on human life, and many other religions have noticeably wider concerns with the sacredness or value of life, and with the wrongness of killing. That offshoot of Hinduism, the religion of the Jains, goes furthest, in asking its followers to allow their own deaths rather than take any life at all. Nor, importantly, should we stop at religion. Atheists and agnostics will often admit to a belief in the sanctity of life, and even if the term 'sacred' seems to insist on an explicitly religious connection, the related notions of reverence and respect are available as secular counterparts. So it seems unjustifiably pedantic to insist on a specifically religious, or specifically Christian interpretation to ideas of sanctity. We should accept that language can be a bit loose, and not attempt to tie it down with artificial constraints and limitations.

I'll come back to religious views a bit later on, but for now it might seem that we're back at square one, with a big spread of views and nothing to choose between them. But that's not quite right. Remember, what we're really after here is finding out what beliefs in the sanctity of life have going for them. That's more important than finding out what the phrase 'life is sacred' really means. Maybe there just is no one thing that it really means. What we can do, though, is look at some of the suggested interpretations of that phrase, and then ask, given that interpretation, what reasons are there for thinking the phrase is true? And we can focus on just a pair of accounts, both of them apparently plausible, and both of them fairly widely supported, and see what they're about. It's going to be useful to choose accounts with a fair bit of contrast between them, so we'll do just that.

A Reverence for Life

We can start with this, as it's the easier to deal with. It's the view about sanctity that I attributed to Albert Schweitzer. The idea is that all living things are valuable, not for what they can do for us, or for each other, but in themselves. And so it's wrong to kill things without good reason, and generally regrettable when things die, especially when they die prematurely.

This isn't an extreme view. As I've sketched it here, the emphasis is on not killing, rather than actively bringing new life into existence. And it doesn't say that killing is so awful that we must never do it. Even if Jains are theoretically committed to starving to death, still, there is no need to follow them down that route: we can have reverence in the sense intended here even while eating, in moderation, when we need to. But even if it isn't extreme, it's a view with problems.

The first has just been hinted at. This is really a bit loose and sloppy view, and it's hard to pin down what precisely it comes to. While most of us will want to agree that killing without good reason is wrong, we'll very likely disagree about just which reasons are good, and therefore disagree about when killing is justified, and when reverence is displayed. Now if, as I think, most of these questions about life and death are complex and many layered, that sort of disagreement might not only be expected, but also welcome. The problem, though, is that talk of sanctity and reverence sounds a bit like sloganeering – we're led by these phrases to expect clear-cut distinctions, only then to have these expectations dashed. If a view is going to be loose and sloppy, if it's going to be, in the end, one that, hedged with qualifications, almost everyone can sign up to, it's surely better to be that way openly from the start, rather than presenting itself as sharp edged.

The second problem is more serious. For what about this case?

> *Hell-bent on Vandalism.* People think of Amber as a nice girl. Her parents lived in a commune in the 1960s and she's picked up a lot of their gentle, softly spoken, and peace-loving ways. But she has this darker side. She likes to smash things up, sometimes as a release, when she's angry, sometimes just for the fun of it. Yet she's been taught to have reverence for life, and so she won't pull the cat's tail, or trample the daffodils. What does she do? She goes into a cave, in deepest Derbyshire, and breaks up the stalactites.

Is it alright for anyone to do this? Maybe you think it is, and think that stalactites don't much matter. But maybe you think that nettles and ants don't much matter either. And stalactites, a thousand times rarer, might still matter more. What's not easy is to agree that it's alright for Amber to go in for destruction of this kind, and yet to urge her against all forms of killing. What's not easy, that is, is to think there's anything particularly distinctive about life. Stalactites aren't alive, but that doesn't immediately make them seem any the less important than some of the things that are. And perhaps Schweitzer doesn't, in the end, think there's anything particular distinctive about life, either. He wrote:

> A man is really ethical only when he obeys the constraint laid on him to help all life which he is able to succour, and when he goes out of his way to avoid injuring anything living. He does not ask how far this or that life deserves sympathy as valuable in itself, nor how far it is capable of feeling. To him life as such is sacred. He shatters no ice crystal that sparkles in the sun, tears no leaf from its tree, breaks off no flower, and is careful not to crush any insect as he walks. If he works by lamplight on a summer evening, he prefers to keep the window shut and breathe stifling air, rather than to see insect after insect fall on his table with singed and sinking wings.

Leaves, flowers, insects might all be alive, but ice crystals certainly aren't. So if we should go out of our way to preserve them, it must be more than life that we're concerned with. So is it the whole of nature? Perhaps it is, and perhaps Schweitzer recognizes here that if we are concerned with life beyond the stage where feelings are in the frame, then there's little reason to insist on a firm boundary between life and non-life. And quite a few people think that the thoughtless, unnecessary and yet wilful destruction of natural things is something we should avoid, whether they're alive or not. Ice crystals, rock formations, sand dunes, distant planets and stars are all of them things that we shouldn't break, or kick around, or cover with junk from rockets.

But then why stop here? It's tempting to think that a blanket disregard for made things (things made by animals – birds' nests, beavers' dams – and things made by human beings, including walls, temples, cities) is also something to object to, even when those made things have been abandoned and no longer serve any use. Here too frivolous, thoughtless, unnecessary destruction is something we should avoid.

I'm certainly not suggesting that we shouldn't in some sense or other respect or revere life, shouldn't in this way think of it as sacred. But the point is that if we are to think of life as something we shouldn't frivolously end, we ought to think of nature and artefacts the same way. Perhaps it is just a general respect for things that we should encourage. Once again, the particular and distinctive substance of this view is dribbling though our fingers.

A Ban on Killing

The second account to be considered is focused just on human beings. And so it's a lot narrower in its range. But it's much stronger in its command. Forget carelessness, frivolity, wanton destruction as things to avoid. Forget too all the fine points about good and bad reasons. It's black and white. Human life is sacred. And we should never bring it to an end – full stop.

Ask people what they understand by the sanctity of life, whether or not they believe in it, and, if there's an answer at all, it will most likely be along these lines. It has supporters and opponents both in large numbers. But those who find this view hard to swallow do not, of course, want *carte blanche* to do away with whomever, whenever, they choose. Most people think that killing human beings is wrong in almost all cases.

But many disagree with sanctity believers about why it's wrong. And they think there are circumstances in which killing can be justified. What circumstances? If we can be clear about just where people want to dissent from this sanctity view, we will, at the same time, be clearer about the view itself.

Make a distinction, first, between factors that lie outside, and those that lie inside the life in question. Look outside, and you might think it is sometimes possible to kill one to save many, or kill a foetus to save the mother, or kill a friendless and more or less useless person to save a scientific genius who is at the same time the life and soul of every party. These are all controversial claims, but I don't think they're particularly interesting here. And this is because it's possible in each case to agree that the life to be ended is valuable, even if you insist nevertheless that it is less valuable than the life, or lives to be saved. This cost-benefit or balance sheet approach can agree that lives have value of the same kind, even if they turn out to be valuable to different degrees. More interesting, because more challenging to the sanctity view, is the claim that some lives – some human lives – might be ended not because they are somewhat less valuable than other lives but because they are not of value at all. In such lives, some people will say, the sorts of circumstances that normally give life its value are altogether missing. And so it might not be at all a bad thing, and might even be a good thing, if such lives are ended.

Three sorts of case need to be considered here. In the first, the human life is allegedly not yet of value, even if it will be of value in the future. In the second, the life is of no value now, even though it was in the past. In the third case, the life is not now, never was, and never will be of value. These three cases correspond to real cases that any of us might encounter: (1) certain sorts of abortion cases; (2) cases concerning those with Alzheimer's disease and so-called persistent vegetative states; and (3) those with congenital malformations and defects such as anencephaly, where someone is born without a brain. Now what seems to be true is that the sorts of things that we most evidently value in human life – self-consciousness, ideas of the future and the past, an ability to relate to and to enjoy both the world and other people – are absent from lives like these. So if such lives are valuable nevertheless, their value must have some other kind of explanation. The point can be put more vividly. Some people use the term 'person' not as a synonym for human being, but to pick out those whose lives are marked by self-consciousness, a sense of time, an awareness of others. Give the term this precise meaning and it seems, first, that there might be persons who are not human beings – possibly God, perhaps dolphins or chimpanzees, maybe Martians. And, second, and here more importantly, using 'person' in this sense, it's going to be clear that there are human beings, or human organisms that are not yet, or no longer, or never will be persons. So the question is why these human beings have a special value nevertheless, and a special value that other things – tigers, geese, oaks – do not have. For remember, the sanctity view being considered here holds that human beings are special.

How do we know, though, that these are not persons? Some people object to the science invoked here. They say we cannot be sure that the foetus is not already thinking, that the patient in a coma or a persistent vegetative state is certain never to recover, or that those with congenital brain damage won't improve with help. But although there are difficult cases, cases in which there can be doubt about what is or will be going on, often this is just clutching at straws. In many cases we do know enough about the workings and failures of the brain to know that thinking, self-consciousness, and standard human responses to the world are altogether absent.

Another kind of objection insists that important facts have not been given their proper weight. The normal foetus, they say, is a *potential* person, something that in the normal run of nature will develop into someone like you and me, and thus will then be valuable. Conversely, those with Alzheimer's or who are severely and irreversibly comatose *were* fully fledged persons, and so were of value. And anencephalics are undoubtedly members of a species whose normal members are persons. There's little point in arguing with any such claims, for they are all certainly true, but the problem, for the sanctity believer, is to explain why and how they are relevant. So she was a person with a valuable life. Why is that a reason for thinking her life is of value now?

One distinction that we drew earlier comes into play here. Critics of the sanctity view will agree that life has, often, more than instrumental value. But, many of them want to say, life is of no personal value in cases like these. Foetuses, anencephalics, those with Alzheimer's disease, or in some irreversible coma, neither want, nor have an interest in staying alive. Life isn't good for them. So why, in such cases, is killing wrong? Believers in life's sanctity have two ways they might respond. They might argue, first, that life is always good for those whose life it is. Maybe there's something in this where a normal healthy foetus is concerned, but it's a less convincing response in the other cases. Or they might insist, instead, that whether or not it is of personal value is beside the point. For life, and in particular human life, is intrinsically valuable, valuable just in itself, no matter what.

Another sort of case still needs to be considered. It also involves this distinction about value, and will throw light on, and pose problems for, the sanctity view. Think about the cases discussed so far, where someone is not, in the sense outlined, a person. I've suggested that it isn't easy to see how such lives have value. And these non-persons cannot themselves have a view about the value of their lives. In other cases lives maybe do have value. And views about that value can be expressed.

> *Wanting Out.* Driving to California, José and Ramon crash on the interstate freeway. Some people say they were going too fast, some blame the truck driver, others say it was just one of those things. They survive, but their injuries are horrific, both in near-constant pain, unable to work or look after themselves, José in a wheelchair, and Ramon confined for the remainder of his days to a hospital bed. Things don't get better. José decides, eventually, to throw himself from the Golden Gate Bridge. Ramon, though, can neither help nor harm himself. He asks the doctor if he can do anything to bring his life to an end.

José and Ramon have a lot in common. They are both persons – both, in spite of their injuries, still self-conscious thinking beings. And they are both able at times to get some small pleasures out of life – their lives are not unremitting agony from one day to the next. But they both believe their lives are, on balance, no longer worth living, and they want them to be over. The difference is that while José is able by himself to end his life, Ramon cannot do this, and needs, if he is to get what he wants, the help of others.

Many believers in the sanctity of life will object to both deaths. Even if there are reasons to make a legal distinction, allowing suicide, while prohibiting euthanasia, the cases are morally on a par. It is wrong to kill others, whether or not they want to die, and it is wrong too to kill ourselves. But why is it wrong? If you subscribe to this sanctity view, then you'll insist that José and Ramon are making some kind of mistake in wanting things to end. Even if there are many bad things about their lives, and even if they'll never improve, still something of considerable value is being overlooked. Either it is good for them to continue living, or, even if it isn't good for them, it's good just in itself that these lives should continue. Their lives are of either personal, or intrinsic value. But there are, I think, real problems with both of these claims. It's certainly true that people can make mistakes about the value of their lives, exaggerating the bad and neglecting the good, or looking to the short term and forgetting the long. And, falsely believing that life is no longer worth living, people can end their lives when, it seems, it would have been better for them to continue. Romeo was right to be upset when, after their plan went wrong, he found Juliet seemingly dead. But she wasn't to die for. Nor was he. Both of them would have got over it. Chatterton, too, almost certainly over-reacted when he took his failure as a poet so much to heart, and ended his life at 18. But equally, people can get it right. There are cases where there's just not enough of value in someone's life to compensate and counter the bad, and where it really isn't in any way good for them to go on living. Maybe it's like this for José and Ramon. Maybe pain, frustration, the hopelessness of the future is all so much that they're right to think they'll be better off dead.

Yet if believers in life's sanctity accept this, and shift to the other view, stressing intrinsic rather than personal value, then their position seems yet more harsh. Can we really believe that even if someone's life is thoroughly wretched, does nothing for them, will never improve, they should, in spite of their strong and considered wish to the contrary, go on living? And that they should do this because it is somehow good just in itself, or good for the universe that their lives continue? It's not simply that this view is harsh. And my worry isn't just that I don't see how this good for the universe can outweigh the bad for the person, it's the bigger worry that this notion of the intrinsic value of life makes no sense at all.

Religion Revisited

I said we'd come back to religion. For some people will object that this aspect of the sanctity view is being ignored. Look at things from the religious perspective and, the suggestion goes, both the distinctiveness of human life, and the outright ban on killing can more easily be explained.

There are various points to be made. First, religious believers often say that what makes us special is that we alone have souls. Moreover, we all have souls, no matter how young, old, under-developed, decrepit, or incapacitated we are. A lot of people doubt whether this is true, and even among themselves Christians have puzzled and argued about exactly when a soul attaches itself to a foetus. But even if we assume there are souls, and that they are present in human bodies for the duration, not much is done for the sanctity view. For believers in souls, Christians and non-Christians alike, often think that the soul is in some way trapped in the body, and will be released from this often unhappy confinement at the moment of death. Socrates held such a view, centuries before Jesus was born, and believed for that reason his death wouldn't be the tragedy that others feared. So even if it might be a bad thing, were it possible, to destroy a man's soul, the value of the soul doesn't give us any reason not to destroy his body.

Another religious view is that life is a gift from God, and not ours to end. So we show a lack of respect for this gift if we bring about the death of a human life, no matter what its condition. But this isn't altogether clear. First, if it's really a gift, and not something that's simply on loan, it's presumably ours to do with as we wish. More important, perhaps, if human life is a gift, so too is animal and plant life. But we are permitted, most people and most Christians believe, to end those lives.

The religious perspective has one more attempt. Human beings, and they alone, are all made, and all equally made, in the image of God. It's this that sets our lives apart from animal and plant life. And it's this that explains why our ending a human life is in effect an attack on God. But this view is hard to swallow. It's hard to see how the differences between human lives, especially the differences between persons and non-persons, are merely superficial, and that there is beneath them something of equal value, or equal worth. And it may even be tempting to echo the near blasphemous thoughts of David Hume, in his *Dialogues Concerning Natural Religion*, and to think that if God really did make us all in his image, then he's not much of a craftsman.

Perhaps these arguments have more merit than I'm suggesting, or perhaps religion has other things to say that might explain why killing human beings is always wrong. But, obviously, one of the problems for any of these arguments is that they'll only work for people who themselves adopt the religious perspective on life. If sanctity views have to depend on religion, then they're unlikely to win the day.

Is Life Sacred?

Where does this leave us? Some of what I've said here is controversial, but none of it is quite as controversial as it may seem. Again, the temptation, and one to be avoided, is to see things as more clear-cut, more black and white, than in fact they are. In arguing against some sanctity of life views I haven't wanted to suggest that life is of no value, or that there should be no restrictions on killing. There are, and should be, many such restrictions. Even in those cases where human beings aren't persons, there are lots of reasons for thinking that life should continue, lots of reasons for not ending life. That people want children is a reason to have them, and a reason to give foetuses some protection under the law. That relatives will be distressed if someone in a persistent vegetative state is allowed to die does have a bearing on whether that life should continue. And that we would all feel less secure if people with Alzheimer's disease were routinely terminated, once personhood disappeared, is an argument against euthanasia. But these reasons don't appeal to the intrinsic or the personal value of human life. So they don't connect with views about sanctity. And reasons like these are not so weighty that they immediately overrule any competing reasons. So they don't offer the straightforward answers to moral dilemmas that many sanctity views promise to deliver.

Why so negative about sanctity? Perhaps it's already clear. I think there really are a lot of good questions about life and death. Many views about the sanctity of life provide neat and pat answers to these questions. But they are too neat, too pat, and make the questions less good. They remove work that needs to be done.

The main point of this chapter, then, has not been simply to clear things up, even though some things are, I hope, now clearer than they were. Rather, its point has been more to resist attempts, via an appeal to the sanctity of life, to clear things up. If things aren't so often black and white, if they're rarely neat and pat, then we have no option, in thinking about matters of life and death, to look at a range of issues on a case-by-case basis. And that's what we'll do.

Chapter Three

Is It Bad to Die?

He who pretends to look on death without fear lies. All men are afraid of dying, this is the great law of sentient beings, without which the entire human species would soon be destroyed.

(Jean-Jacques Rousseau, *La Nouvelle Héloïse*)

Think of all the dreadful things that might happen to you, and dying is very likely to be among them. For some of us this is as bad as it gets, nothing could be worse, and life in any condition is better. For others, and maybe most, it's certainly a bad thing, even if it might be better to die than to be tortured, or to have your children murdered in front of you. This attitude to death is borne out by our reactions to the news and events around us – war is more terrible the greater the number of fatalities, car crashes in which people are killed get more coverage than those in which they are injured, capital punishment is worse than imprisonment. It's borne out, too, by our own immediate responses to dangerous situations. If we didn't think death was bad, there'd be no point in stepping out of the way of buses, or queuing for hours to see a doctor, or following the safety instructions after boarding a plane. And if we didn't think death was bad, we'd find it hard to understand what's going on, for much of the time, in films, and literature, and painting.

But is this all a mistake? Is death really bad, or is the whole idea that it is based on a misunderstanding, something that happens when we think about death in the wrong way, something that we ought to give up? Do we all worry too much about death and dying?

Some people have thought that we do, and have insisted that really there is nothing at all to fear in, because there's nothing at all bad about, death. Death, they say, is just not the evil it's typically made out to be. But before thinking about how this strange view gets argued, and who those people are who argue for it, it's important to get clear about just what is being claimed, when it's claimed that death isn't bad. And to get clear about this we need, once again, to make a number of distinctions.

Let's get these distinctions in place now, at the outset, and it will be easier to stay clear later.

Some Distinctions

First, then, distinguish dying from being dead. Dying is a process, often long and drawn out, and too often painful, that we undergo while alive. Indeed, only the living can be dying. It's a process, of course, that usually ends in death. (Usually, I think, because someone who is really dying, say, through loss of blood, can sometimes be saved from death.) And being dead itself is a state in which we'll all, sooner or later, end up. You might think that we shift from dying to being dead without ado. Or you might think that there is a split second event – the moment of death itself that takes us from one to the other. This isn't so important. What matters is the distinction here between what there is in life, the process of dying, and what there is after life, the state of being dead.

Next, distinguish between different ways of being dead. Assume first – what most of us already believe – that death is forever, and that no one and nothing will bring us back to life. And then assume as well – and this again is something that many people believe anyway – that death, and being dead, is a sort of nothingness. Assume, in other words, that there is no afterlife of the kinds that religions threaten or promise, no paradise with virgins, no heaven or hell, no walking the earth in some sort of zombie fashion, no transformation into a vampire. And if it's nothingness, then when dead, there is no memory of your previous life, no hopes for the future, no pleasure or pain, and no awareness of being dead. So death is really the end – once dead, forever dead, and for you, at least, all events, thoughts, feelings, are over and done with.

Finally, distinguish between the different people who might be involved. There's the dead person, on the one hand, and those left behind, on the other. For the dead there's nothing, while for the living – friends, enemies, relatives, onlookers, fans – there is grief, regret, disappointment, indifference, relief, and a host more reactions besides. Their situation is quite different from that of the person who has died.

With these distinctions in place, it's easier to focus down on the question that we want to address. Dying itself might well be bad; being dead, if there is a hell with fires and torment, might even be worse; and certainly the death of one person can have terrible consequences for those left behind – remember how many were upset when John Lennon was shot, or how, at the start of the First World War, the assassination of Franz Ferdinand led to events in which millions were killed. But the question we're thinking about here contrasts with all of this. The question is about whether, assuming for now that it's nothingness, death is bad for the person who dies. So imagine . . .

> *Not a Fairy-tale Ending.* Young lovers. A candlelit dinner on the river bank. Cool jazz, oysters, champagne. They're planning their future together. It's late, and she falls asleep in the car driving her home. But then someone steps into the road, the car swerves, loses control, hits the bridge, overturns. She is killed outright, instantly. The others, miraculously, survive.

This case is, of course, like a real one of some years ago. But in this imagined case there is no room for doubt about the rosy future, or the suddenness of death. That makes things clearer. We can assume here too that this woman's death is a great shock to everyone, her family are devastated, friends grieve, even strangers leave flowers at the sight of the crash, and outside her home. But still we can ask, does anything bad happen to her?

A lot of us will think it does. There she is, young, beautiful, everything to live for. And suddenly she's gone. Or a case I heard about only today – two Iranian lawyers, 29, twins, joined at the head. They both die, still under anaesthetic, when, in its late stages, the operation to separate them goes wrong. To be cut off, annihilated, cancelled, to lose that future, that promise, isn't that obviously a terrible thing? Who would want to deny this? And why?

Against the Badness of Death

Maybe they were just reputation seekers, out to promote utterly controversial views, denying what seemed to most people to be blindingly obvious. Yet more likely they were sincere, and had, or thought they had, good reasons to back up their position. But Epicurus, a philosopher from ancient Greece, and Lucretius, a Roman follower some centuries later, both insisted that our fear of death is irrational, and that death isn't bad for us. It's known as the Epicurean view of death. But why believe it, and how, if at all, could they argue for it?

It connects with, and arises from, a pair of quite general beliefs which they both held. First, Epicurus and Lucretius were *atomists* – long before there was any scientific support for such a view, they believed that all that there is in the universe are particles of stuff, combinations of such particles, and the spaces between the particles. Or, as their predecessor, Democritus, put it, nothing other than atoms and the void. And it's because they were in this sense atomists that Epicurus and Lucretius were able to believe that after death we effectively cease to exist, and so that death, and being dead, are effectively nothing to us. Think of a television, or a mobile phone. It starts with minor faults, becomes increasingly unreliable, and then breaks down completely. Either in frustration or because it's no more than it deserves, you pulverise it. Even though you end up with a handful of dust, for the atoms remain, the TV, the phone, are there no longer. This, for atomists, is how it is for us in death.

Second, they were also *hedonists*. That can seem a loaded term, and even today we still sometimes talk of an Epicurean as someone given to high living, fine wine, rich food, luxury. But although there's some connection, hedonists aren't simply crude pleasure seekers. Not crude, for as well as the more glaring examples there are subtler and longer lasting pleasures that you might enjoy – maybe music, and friendship, and learning that sparrows are not becoming extinct. And not simple, for hedonists are as much concerned with avoiding pain as with finding pleasure, and one of the problems with some of the cruder or more obvious pleasures is that they bring pain in their wake. But there are subtler as well as more obvious pains that need to be considered, and frustration, grief, anxiety are all bad for us, and count against the good life, just as surely as do hangovers, grazed knees and arthritis. Nor are hedonists simply out for number one – it's good to give pleasure to others, as well as to get it for yourself. What they want to insist on, though, is, first, that doing good is doing good for someone or something, and, second, that things are good for someone or something when and only when they add to, or take from, pleasure and pain. So good and bad connects with feeling. And now as, when dead, we feel nothing – nothing good, nothing bad – so death cannot be bad for us. Or as Epicurus puts it:

> Accustom thyself to believe that death is nothing to us, for good and evil imply sentience, and death is the privation of all sentience . . . Death, therefore, the most awful of evils, is nothing to us. When we are, death is not come, and when death is come, we are not. It is nothing, then, either to the living or the dead, for with the living it is not, and the dead exist no longer.

It's a mistake, then, given these views, to think that our young woman in any way suffers or is harmed by her death. Dying is sudden, and without pain. It's unexpected, and there's no fear or anxiety beforehand. Others grieve, but she is oblivious to this. She is dead and so she feels, and will feel, nothing. And so nothing bad has happened to her.

There's another strand to the argument. Lucretius asks us to think about two periods of non-existence, the time before we're born, and the time after our death. Almost no one wishes they were born earlier; or thinks there's anything bad about this earlier period of non-existence. But then it seems irrational and inconsistent to hope we might die later, and to think there's anything bad about not existing in the later period. Both periods are, for us, equally devoid of awareness and sensation, pleasure and pain, and both periods lie equally beyond the boundaries of our lives. So far as we are concerned, there's nothing to choose between them.

Who Can Believe It?

The Epicureans wanted to make life better. And they thought that if we could see the truth about death, we would be able to approach our own demise in a different way, calmer, less anxious, no longer afraid.

Is this, though, a lesson we can really hope to learn? Or are they going to have their work cut out in trying to persuade others of their views? One thing to notice here is that while hedonism, in some form or other, might seem to be relatively common, atomism certainly isn't. Even if for a handful of Greeks they had a theoretical existence, most people in the history of the world have never even heard of atoms. And even if many people today believe atoms exist, only a few of us are atomists, believing that's all there is – a lot of people think there are gods, or spirits, or souls as well. Remove all the atoms from the universe and it won't follow that there are no gods. Separate or destroy the atoms in someone's body, and it doesn't follow that the spirit or soul will disappear. And so this Epicurean view is only going to work, at best, for people who believe that death is really the end, and who've given up on stories of the afterlife. It didn't work for many Greeks or Romans, most of whom were religious in one way or another, and it didn't really work through two thousand years of Christianity, when spirits and souls, heaven and hell were taken more or less for granted. There've been some exceptions. Shakespeare's Hamlet, in his famous soliloquy, tussles with the question of whether suicide will bring him nothingness, or whether afterwards there will be some kind of experience, and some kind of price to pay. At around the same time, in France, Montaigne wrote in his essays about death as if it's a kind of annihilation. In the eighteenth century David Hume scandalized Boswell by his show of equanimity in the face of his imminent demise. And at the beginning of the last century Wittgenstein seems to have been consciously echoing the Epicurean view in the gnomic utterance of his *Tractatus*, 'Death is not an event in life.' Discussion of Epicureanism is becoming more widespread recently, as conventional religious beliefs find it harder to survive, and thinking about the puzzles of life and death is freed from earlier constraints. Even so, it has still only handfuls of takers.

Some Puzzles

Yet maybe you're one of them. Maybe you were already someone who doesn't worry, and thinks there's no reason to worry, about death. Or maybe, having come across the Epicurean view, you're immediately convinced. But it's perhaps much more likely that you suspect there's something not quite right about it. And something not quite right, even if, like most atheists, you accept that death is the end, and that there's nothing beyond. Atheists are as likely to be as unhappy about death as believers, with many of them finding little consolation in the thought that there's an eternity of nothingness ahead. Take Philip Larkin, for example, eaten up by thoughts of his extinction through most of his life, and increasingly so towards the end. In his late poem, 'Aubade', he first packs off conventional religion – 'that vast moth-eaten musical brocade/ Created to pretend we never die' before rubbishing the Epicureans. For theirs is:

> . . . specious stuff that says *No rational being*
> *Can fear a thing it will not feel*, not seeing
> That this is what we fear – no sight, no sound,
> No touch or taste or smell, nothing to think with,
> Nothing to love or link with,
> The anaesthetic from which none come round.

So how do the Epicureans respond? There's no point denying either that this fear of death is for many people real, or that it is bad for us to feel it. But, they'll want to insist, it is an irrational fear nevertheless, and one that, if we think things through, ought to disappear. And Larkin goes wrong, or so they'll say, in not really seeing what is implied by his phrase, 'nothing to think with'. Without that, his vision is truly horrifying – like being buried alive; or like having an operation when the anaesthetic only half works, and stops you from screaming, but lets you feel the pain. But if you have faith in anaesthetics, then it's crazy to worry about this. And if you really believe in nothingness, it's similarly crazy to worry about death. Yes, it is like a permanent anaesthetic. And if you were all the time wanting to come round that would be a problem. But you won't be.

There's going to be a suspicion, too, about their account of grief. Agreed, we shouldn't confuse the situation of the dead person with that of the survivors, but if it is reasonable to feel grief when someone dies, then surely this suggests that death is bad for that person. The Epicureans, though, allow a space for grief, and the legitimacy of feelings of regret, distress, a sense of loss. But then they insist that the loss is ours. Just as it was both natural and rational to feel such emotions, in days before jets and the internet, if someone emigrated to Australia, so also with death. There's a finality to both partings, and for those left behind the need to come to terms with this. The hope, of course, for those boarding the ship, was that life in a new country would be good for them. There can't be this hope about death. But, unlike with Australia, there is at least the certainty, assuming nothingness, that this new state won't be bad for them. If we think, in feeling grief, that the dead might themselves have lost out, might now be having a miserable time, then again we are wrong.

Another objection makes us think more about hedonism. Feeling pleasure is good. And feeling pain is bad. But feeling less pleasure than you did is bad as well. Maybe it won't spoil your holiday completely, and there'll still be things to do, but if it's sunny the first week, and raining the next, then the amount of pleasure you get will be reduced. And that's bad. And surely death is bad in the same way. It doesn't feel bad to be dead. But death puts an end to pleasure, and the good things in life. And that is what is bad about it.

But, again the Epicureans have a reply. In the normal case, you are aware that your pleasure is less, and this is frustrating or irritating. At the very least, you think it's a pity it's still raining. And it's because of these kinds of feelings, this awareness, that we'll take this line about a drop in pleasure. But of course all such awareness is missing after we die. And so even though it's a pleasure-free zone, and a successor to what is, in many cases, a good life, there's nothing bad in death.

Experience

All this seems to suggest, what may have been suggested already, that the Epicureans are appealing, in their view about death, to the old adage, what you don't know can't harm you. But is this actually true, or is it just one of those things people say, without really thinking it through? I think there's something in it. But if we try to find just what that something is, then, I'm going to suggest, we'll find a first weakness in the Epicureans' position.

Some things that you don't know can harm you, either because you'll find out about them later, or because you'll find out about their effects. You don't know, and maybe will never know, that I've spiked your drink, but you'll feel the headache when it comes, and I've certainly harmed you. But contrast this situation with another:

> *Fated.* She's young, happy, successful. Stella has, it seems, everything to live for. She's a star at work, with her copy somehow always satisfying even the most exacting of their clients. Hardly surprising that she's first choice for their international assignments. Next week she's off to Rio. There's only one problem. Already she has the beginnings of a disease that, in three or four years, is certain to kill her. It doesn't, however. Before any symptoms develop, before anyone, doctors included, has the slightest inkling, she's killed in a plane crash. This disease, that would have had devastating effects had she lived, has, because of the quite unrelated accident, been effectively short-changed.

Was it bad for Stella to have the disease? Was she harmed by it? Perhaps this is one of those questions to which there isn't a clear-cut answer, but at least we can well enough understand someone who says, in this sort of case, that nothing bad happened, and there was no harm. It's in this sort of case, then, that we might accept that the adage is true.

Does this help with the Epicurean view on death? A bit, but its supporters go wrong if they think the disease case exactly parallels that of death. For there's this important difference. The whole course of Stella's life, so far as she and others are aware, runs exactly the same way whether she has the disease or not. She has neither more pleasures or pains, good times or bad, as a result of the infection. It makes no difference whatsoever to her experience. Not so with death. Of course you're not aware of it, but death puts an end, forever, to your experience. So it makes a massive difference.

Epicureans can insist that this massive difference isn't really important, and that you're no more harmed by death than is Stella by her disease. They can insist that only differences that you are, or will be aware of, count. But why believe them?

Parallels

Another way you might undermine the Epicureans is to point out certain counter-intuitive or far-fetched aspects of their view. This won't prove they're wrong, for something far-fetched might nevertheless be true, but it should put them on the defensive.

It's well worth emphasizing, first of all, that their view in its entirety is pretty hard to swallow. Death isn't bad. Isn't that already absurd? So it's not as though we're looking here for some unpalatable implications of a position which, taken just in itself, seems fair enough.

And then the view has certain curious consequences. For the Epicureans need to say that not only is death not bad for us, neither too is it bad to fall into a coma from which you never recover, or into a persistent vegetative state. It would, of course, be bad, as with so-called locked-in syndrome, to appear to be in a coma and yet all the time be conscious of the world outside. A French journalist, Jean-Dominique Bauby, was in this situation a few years ago. We know about it only because he could still blink in one eye, this was eventually noticed, and on this basis communication was restored. It would be bad too, because of the distress you'd feel about the lost years, to be in a coma for a decade and then eventually to come round. And it's bad for the relatives. But think just about the person in a genuine, deep and irreversible coma. As with death, there's no awareness, no sentience, no pleasures and pains. So, like death, it cannot, on the Epicurean view, be bad for the person con-cerned. Now someone might think I've got the Epicureans wrong here, for they seem to want to put emphasis on their claim that the dead don't exist, while the comatose certainly do. But I'm sure it must be the point about non-feeling, a mental non-existence, rather than disappearance of the body (which is after all in most cases only gradual) that carries the weight of their argument. And so they will be as blasé about comas as they are about death.

Yet this is odd. Suppose your sister is in a coma, but you could, if you wanted to, somehow revive her. If you do, she'll resume her normal life with no ill-effects. If you don't, she'll remain in the coma for thirty years and then die. You would, I think, find it bizarre if someone suggested that you ought really to leave her be, as there's nothing at all bad about a permanent coma, while there is something bad about one that ends. But then if there is reason to bring her round, and the sooner the better, then there is reason, if you can help it, not to allow her to go in a coma in the first place. And if that's right, then there are, equally, reasons to avoid death.

Here's another one. If the Epicureans are right, and there can be nothing bad in death, then there can be nothing good in it either. If it's irrational always to fear or to shun death, then it's irrational also to embrace, or welcome it. But it's hard to believe this. A lot of people think that it can, in some circumstances, be better to die than to live. We can think this about wounded animals, when we put them out of their misery. And even if there are reservations about euthanasia, it's hard not to think that present pain and future prospects together might be such that for someone's life to end is better, and better for them, than for it to continue. But on the Epicurean view, thoughts like these must be muddled. You think you should shoot the fox that's being torn apart by hounds? The Epicurean comes along and tells you not to waste the bullet. As death is nothing, the fox can't be better off dead. You'll agree that it won't feel better being dead, it won't be aware the pain is over, and it won't thank you for ending its life. Even so, in this situation not feeling is better – and better for the fox – than feeling. So it can be better to die than to live. But surely, if this is right, it can equally be worse to die than to live. And so the Epicurean view, in insisting that death isn't bad, has got to be wrong.

The Epicureans could just dig in. They could just insist that there's nothing bad about death, nothing bad about comas, and nothing good about them either. They could insist that there are just no comparisons to be made between states in which we are, or will be, aware of things, ourselves included, and states in which we aren't, and won't. That's one option. Another is to make some concessions. So perhaps the Epicureans will now suggest the following distinction: states such as death, or a coma, might indeed be worse, or better than life, but even so they cannot, in themselves, be good or bad. Such states can have a relative value, but they cannot have any absolute value.

Does this make sense? It does, I think, make sense of a kind. We might agree that considered just in itself being dead, or being in a coma, is neither good nor bad, with nothing good or bad happening to someone in such a state. But to agree with this is simply to agree to a point long conceded, that being dead, assuming it's nothingness, won't involve good or bad feelings, sensations, or experiences. There's nothing new here. And if the Epicureans are prepared to give in on the further point, and agree that you can be better off, or worse off when dead, then they've given in on the major issue. For there's no longer any important difference between them, and their opponents. Think about someone who has a small house, a wife, a young child. It's not a bad life. But last year he lost almost all his money when his business went bust, and his two older children when he hit a truck on the freeway. It's a worse life. And even if your situation isn't bad, just in itself, it is bad to be much worse off than you were. There are reasons to avoid, beforehand, and to regret, afterwards, any substantial decline in your fortune.

Death and Deprivation

If you can be worse off dead, then there are reasons to avoid life-threatening situations, reasons to regret death, reasons to grieve over lives lost, reasons to be worried that soon you might die, and so on. This is all anyone wanted. All anyone wanted, then, can be captured in what is known as the *deprivation view*, the view that death is bad not because of any positive qualities – for nothingness has, in itself, no qualities either way – but because of what it deprives us of. It's because death puts an end, often, to a good life, that it is, often, bad to die. So Epicurus goes wrong in focusing just on the internal qualities of death, or non-existence, and ignoring the all-important relation to the life it ends. And note that it's possible now to reply to Lucretius, when he argues that as pre-natal non-existence isn't bad, neither is post-mortem non-existence. We can agree that considered just in themselves, these states are the same, and of neutral value. Nevertheless death deprives us, often, of a good life, while nothing similar can be said about not existing before you were born. So they are importantly different after all.

The deprivation view might seem straightforward, but in fact there are various details that need more thinking about. I'm going to hold back on most of this until the next chapter. Right now I just want to look at one point that the deprivation view seems to imply, but which many of us will still not be happy about.

Celebrations. Clarrie's been ill for months now. Of course, no one really knows what started it, but some people say that it's probably one of those mixes they used on the farm years ago, when she was still a girl. Most of them have been banned since then. But there's nothing to be done about the past. Not much about the future either. The doctors agree it's hopeless, just a matter of time. And each day the pain seems to get worse. It's terrible, and everyone's hoping for the end. It comes on Tuesday, just after 7 o'clock. Her family are all there. And how do they react? They wipe away the tears, put on some music, open the champagne, and celebrate.

But people don't react like this. No matter how bad the life, we can't simply be pleased when someone we care about dies. There's relief, of course, that it's all over, and we might well think that she's better off dead, given how things were towards the end.

There's something still not quite right about the deprivation view, then. We don't seem to think that death, just in itself, is neutral, and takes whatever value it has from the life it ends. Certainly we think it bad when it ends a good life, but we don't, in fact, think it's good when it ends a bad life. It still seems, to most of us, to be a bad thing either way. Can this be right?

It might seem that it can, but it isn't easy, I think, to spell it out. Death may be better than a life of agony, but it's not better than a good life. And we might think there's nothing absolutely inevitable about the life of agony. Clarrie might not have been ill. A child born with severe handicaps might, instead, have been perfectly healthy. And it's a pity these people didn't instead have good lives through and through. So although death, for Clarrie, is better than the life she actually had, it's still much worse than the life she could have had. And when, naturally, we resist thinking that death is a good thing, it's probably because we have this alternative, and better life in mind. Dying is sometimes better than living, but it's always bad, as it always rules out, draws a curtain over, the good life that might have been.

Yet this isn't altogether satisfactory. First, 'might have been' here is used in a very weak sense. We've already agreed her condition was hopeless. It's not as though there might have been a miracle cure. Second, and more important, it seems to cut both ways. Someone lives a good life. We don't think there's something good about their death because their life might have been bad, might have been one not worth living, and their death rules out the possibility of such a life. Not altogether satisfactory, then, but the best, here, that I can do.

Is it Bad to Die?

It's hard not think the Epicureans are on to something. After all, much of what they say about death is, many of us think, true, and importantly true. There is no pain, no frustration, no regret in death. And, unlike anaesthetics and drugs, there's no future price to pay for this oblivion. So it's true that being dead won't feel bad. Admittedly, it's true too that when we are alive, the future matters to us, true that we plan, and as human beings need to plan, to give life some shape. And a lot of our concern with this shaping is perfectly rational. Two things can be separated out here. So, first, just assuming we're going to be alive in the future, it's reasonable now to take some steps to ensure that future is pleasant enough to live through. So it's reasonable to think about next week's shopping, to get the leaky roof fixed before winter, maybe even to continue with the pension plan. These things are reasonable, assuming you'll go on living. But, second, there are very likely reasons now to want to go on living. You really want to finish your second symphony, see how the garden matures, climb all the Scottish Munros. Desires like these give you reason now to stay alive, to exercise, to eat tolerably well, to keep out of the way of buses. Were you suddenly to die, you wouldn't be able to do the things you so much want to do, these things which give shape and meaning to your life. Hence the badness of death. But then were you to die, not only your life, and its shape, but these desires as well would disappear. And when, in this way, everything goes at once, it can sometimes be hard to see what would be bad about it.

So is death bad or not? That's the question, but it isn't easy to give a firm answer. One option is to go along with the Epicureans, and to think that death isn't bad at all. Your situation can't be bad once feeling is at an end. Another is to follow the deprivation account, allow that death is bad, but acknowledge that it's bad in a decidedly non-standard way. Although just in itself the state of being dead doesn't harm us, it is bad if our lives, assuming perhaps that they're more or less good, are cut off when they are only part way through.

It would be better, though, if death didn't stand completely on a limb here, and if there were other things that we can agree are bad, even if they don't lead to anyone's feeling bad. Are there other things? We've thought about the coma – alive but with no feeling. But it doesn't significantly strengthen the argument for death's badness – the Epicureans are likely to reject this case as well. Perhaps there are different examples elsewhere? Some people think it would be bad if great works of art, or great works of nature were destroyed, even if none of us ever regretted that destruction, and the consequent loss. Imagine that Titian, in his glory days, painted even more fine canvases than we now have, but then, a perfectionist and moody, destroyed them before anyone else could see them. Or imagine a nuclear war. Our species is the first to go. And then after us the nightingales and the whales. Later still Venice collapses, rivers and waterfalls run dry, and dust and cloud put an end to sunsets. Some people think that losses like these would be bad, even if they aren't experienced as bad by anyone, or any thing. If you're inclined to agree, inclined to reject hedonism, you're more likely to think that human death is bad, even when not experienced by anyone. Yet you might be suspicious about cases like these, but confident, still, about the badness of death. For, to repeat, while we don't experience our death, it does, by ending it, make a big difference to our experience. These other cases, concerning art and nature, leave our experience untouched. So while we might insist that, even if not experienced, death is bad *for* someone, it seems that with art and nature we have no option but to speak of badness *in itself*. And for many, these differences are big enough to make death's badness more secure. So again, the claim that death is bad isn't likely to get much useful support from these further cases.

Nevertheless, this second option, suggesting that death is bad, yet bad in a non-standard way, is one that I'm inclined to think is right. But certainly, if someone insists on the Epicurean view, it would be easier to think of them as freakish than to prove them wrong.

Chapter Four

Which Deaths Are Worse?

There is nothing I desire more to be informed of, than of the death of men: that is to say, what words, what countenance, and what face they show at their death . . . Were I a composer of books, I would keep a register, commented of the diverse deaths, which in teaching men to die, should after teach them to live.

(Montaigne, *Essays*)

Look at some of Dürer's etchings, read poems by John Donne, visit the catacombs in Rome, and you get a vision of death, bleak, horrible, the great leveller, the fate that awaits us all. But are we right to think of death in this way? Or, in succumbing to such a vision, are we overlooking something of the complexity and variety to death, its nuances and shifting value?

There are two bad reasons for thinking that all deaths are equal. Suppose you think that death is not only bad, not only terrible, but the worst possible thing that can happen to someone. Then you'll very likely think that no death can be worse than any other. For how, if every death is the worst possible thing that can happen to a person, can some deaths be worse? Or suppose you think that while lives differ, deaths are all the same. Death is nothingness, forever, and is precisely that in every case. Hence the leveller. There's nothing to choose between us, once we're dead. And so given this evenness, this monotony to death, you might think that however bad death is, there's just nothing that can make one death worse than any other.

Both these are bad reasons, I think, but in different ways. The first is wrong from the outset – death isn't the worst possible thing. It isn't worse than unending torture. Notice also that my worst possible thing might not be exactly the same as yours. The second, though, is wrong later. Even though there isn't variety in death, we shouldn't think deaths are equally bad. And, indeed, it's pretty clear that most people don't think this, and often think, for example, that dying when you're very old is less bad than being cut down your prime. Think about the Queen Mother, and Princess Di. Or, in cases where the ages are the same, we tend to think the death of someone terminally ill, and in great pain, is less bad than that of someone in good health.

The deprivation view is consistent with our intuitions here. We think deaths aren't equally bad. And this view agrees. We think earlier deaths are worse, and that worse too are those that bring to an end a good, rather than a less good life. And the deprivation view supports this, claiming that the badness of death depends on the life it takes away. So there's a way forward. Two people, both strangers, are in danger. But who to save? What makes one death worse than another? It's simple. As the deprivation view explains, the more you lose, the worse it is. But is that as simple as it sounds? And is it right? There's a number of puzzles about which deaths are worse, and a number of ways in which the deprivation view needs to be clarified and refined.

The Integrated Life

We think that, in general, the sooner you die, the more you lose. So the earlier death is worse. But what about babies? Although most of us agree with the general point, we disagree quite a lot about how bad it is when babies, or very young children die, or when a woman suffers a mis-carriage. Some people think that young lives are the most precious of all, while others find the death of an infant less distressing, easier to bear, easier to get over, than that of someone older. It might seem that the first of these reactions is better, and more in tune with the deprivation view. For if the badness of death depends not so much on the past, the life it ends, but more on the future, the life it prevents, then the younger death should always be worse. In general, and obviously, the younger you are, the more you have ahead. So the earlier the death, the greater the loss.

But there's another way of looking at this, one that supports the second, and perhaps more common reaction, that the death of an infant is in some important respect less bad than that of someone older. Imagine a car crash. The children are killed, while the parents survive. One child, Alice, is 17, well liked at school, a bass player in a rock band, looking forward to time out, to travel, and then to university and a career in medicine. The other, Ben, 15 months, is just beginning to talk. Now one difference between them is that while Ben's future is pretty much open ended, Alice's is already, in several respects, mapped out. As we know just what will be lost, so it seems natural to be more concerned about it. But this isn't the whole story. Imagine we did know what would happen later to Ben. The further difference is that Alice herself is already looking forward to, and planning for this future, has already made an investment in and commitment to this upcoming life. It's what she wants. Ben, of course, is hardly yet able to think beyond his next meal. He doesn't even understand that he has a longer-term future, much less is he able to think about, and decide on, its shape. In this sense the ending of his life, no matter how good it will be, doesn't represent a loss to him.

Although it's bad for young children to die, then, we might with reason think it's less bad than a similar death for an older child, or an adult. Why? Because there's not the same degree of psychological connectedness, or integration, running through their lives. There isn't the same degree of self-awareness, self-concern, or – and this is a related point – awareness of others, and of their concerns, or, again related, awareness of time, and in particular an awareness and interest in one's own past and future, and the ways in which decisions now will bear fruit later. For these reasons we might, and justifiably, regret the infant death less than that of the adult, even though for the infant there are more good years to run.

This point about integration has a bearing, as well, on our reactions to the death of those with Alzheimer's and related degenerative diseases – think not only of Iris Murdoch but also of Ronald Reagan and Bernard Levin. Memory, concentration, behaviour are all badly affected, and the more the disease progresses, the fewer the connections between life now and life as it was in the past. And this present life is itself fragmented, making increasingly less sense, as time goes on, either to the person with the disease or to those others who for personal or professional reasons, have no option but to watch its progress. So consider two people, both 80, one with Alzheimer's disease, the other in good health. They both have, let's say, five years ahead of them. But the death of the one with Alzheimer's is less bad than that of the person whose brain continues to function normally.

Ben's life, an infant's life, is fragmented now. With the onset of Alzheimer's, and similar illnesses, this fragmentation, often, is still in the future. If Ben dies, a worthwhile life will be lost, but this isn't, in an important sense, a loss to him. If someone developing Alzheimer's dies, then a worthwhile life is lost, but it would, because of the disease, be lost anyway.

It's worth considering a further, and different case. Many of us are naturally inclined, or sentimentally reared to think of animal deaths, in many cases, as bad. We grieve over the death of pets, fight tooth and nail against fox-hunting, and go to ridiculous lengths, as I do, to capture and then free mice rather than kill them. But although there is often something wretched and agonizing about their manner of dying, and pain is something about which we are right to be concerned, it has to be asked whether a sudden and painless death is bad for the animal concerned. Human death is bad insofar as an integrated or connected life is lost, but in animals such integration is never fully possible to begin with. So it's not, perhaps, ever bad for them to die. A lot of people might agree with this for some less sophisticated forms of life. It's hard to believe, for example, that there's much going on in oysters and, as with anencephalics, hard to see how a quick death can be bad for them. And there's likely to be strong disagreement, perhaps well-founded, in considering cases at the other end of the spectrum. Gorillas, chimps, orang-utans might have a mental life importantly close to ours. But consider an intermediate case – an otter or a kangaroo. There's intelligence, awareness, responsiveness. But is there self-consciousness, any grasp of past and future? Most people have doubts. And if such animals aren't in any clear sense wanting to live on, if there are no hopes for the future, no plans that their demise will leave unrealized, then it's not clear, I think, how death itself can be bad for them.

Suppose this is right. Even so, we shouldn't be too blasé about animal death. Consider:

Man and Beast. Akiro has a difficult decision to make. He thought it only happened in Westerns, but there really is someone tied to the railtracks, a couple of miles ahead. And it's like a war film, the way there's a heap of dynamite stashed and primed under the bridge. He can blow up the runaway train, and bring about the sudden death of the five hundred donkeys on board, or he can allow it to continue, run over whoever it is, and come to a halt at the next incline. He doesn't have long to think.

What should he do? Some people think there's no question here, and no matter how pleading the donkeys' big eyes and doleful faces, people always come first. But I think there need to be questions about this.

Suppose, first, that you're not persuaded by what I've said above, and you do think it's bad for animals to die. You just think human deaths count for more. Well, perhaps one human being is worth five hundred donkeys, but if both are worth something, then it seems there must be some number of animal deaths that outweighs a single human death.

Perhaps it's a thousand donkeys, or a million. Suppose, though, you do agree with me, and think that sudden death isn't bad for animals. Even so, it's still not clear that human life should always come first. For an animal's death might well be bad in other ways. It might be bad for other animals, particularly the offspring left to fend for themselves. And it might be bad for human beings. There's the donkey owner, and there are lots of donkey admirers, all of whom will lose out if these animals die. And surely that needs to be taken into account. Nor do we get anywhere by supposing that human life is of infinite value, so that, even if animals are worth something, one of us outweighs any number of them. Hardly anyone believes this about human life, for hardly anyone thinks that we should always put human life above human welfare, or well-being, or happiness. Hardly anyone thinks that we should put all our money into the health service, and none at all into pizzas, or holidays, or schools.

There's one point about integrated or connected lives that still might need to be clearer. It links with the distinction I made above between connections within one part of life, on the one hand, and connections across different parts, on the other. Both matter. In some cases death is not bad because life, either before or after this divide, is not fully integrated. But in others integration is present on either side of, but not over the divide. Consider:

> *A Miracle Cure?* Kwame is suffering from a brain tumour. Without treatment he'll die, probably next year, 18 months at the outside. Surgery is an option, but it's risky, and even if he survives, he might well be a semi-invalid thereafter. But now there's a new treatment, a drug therapy that is more or less guaranteed to get rid of the tumour completely, to remove all threat not only of death but of any kind of physical impairment. Mentally, however, it's another story. Although he'll be at least as alert, as able, as active as ever before, Kwame is likely to undergo significant, and sudden, personality changes. Not only may he find that he is no longer suited to his job, he might develop new friends, new politics, a different sense of humour. He'll become, in some familiar sense, a different person.

Should he accept this treatment? Many of us will think not. What we want is for our own lives to continue, not for there to be some life or other, no matter how good, that starts where our own life leads off. And in Kwame's case this is, in some sense, just what happens. It could be worse. I've not suggested that the drug affects his memory, so we can assume that he remembers, after the operation, the things he did before. He remembers, as well, the things that he'd hoped to do, if the operation was a success. But now he finds both that these plans mean nothing to him, and that in looking back, he can't identify with and relate to the person he knows he once was. So if, now, Kwame can anticipate that he'll change in these ways, he may well choose to forego the treatment, and make instead the best of the time he has left. It's bad for him to die, but it's bad, as well, to turn into someone else, or to become a person he cannot, now, much care about.

Sometimes, in similar situations, people have no choice. Those who are, or are alleged to be, mentally ill are often subject to 'cures' which bring about substantial behavioural change. The only exceptional thing about the actress Frances Farmer, and the alterations in her brought about by a frontal lobotomy, was the extent of her fame. But the shift from a lively and intelligent, even if socially maladjusted, young woman to someone lethargic, slow-witted but biddable was nothing uncommon. Particularly in the USA thousands of people were similarly treated, against their will, and with similar results. Even if, afterwards, life is still worth living, the degree of change, coupled with the fact that it is forcibly introduced, is such as to generate serious doubts as to whether this worthwhile life is, for the person to be operated on, in any way better than death.

The Longer Life

We think that the Queen Mother's death was much less bad than that of Princess Diana because she was so much older. She had so many more years behind her, and so few still to go. So, in dying when she did, she lost very little. But isn't there something odd about this? We seem to be saying her death isn't particularly bad because dying, around that time, is more or less inevitable. Yet isn't that bad? Isn't it bad that life is short, and that anyone reaching a hundred has already had many more years than they might have expected?

Some people have thought so. Death in old age might be much more common than death in the prime of life, but, the thought goes, that in itself cannot prevent it from being a very bad thing. Imagine we lived for 500 years. Death at 30 is worse than death at 100, but it's no longer a lot worse. We don't live for 500 years, but that in itself is something we might very much regret.

There's a number of things to sort out here. One involves a distinction between death and deaths. We might think that the Queen Mother's particular death, on such and such a day, wasn't so bad, given the very high probability that she'd die soon in any event, but even so death in general, the very fact that she would soon die, is bad. Or imagine James, 30, killed by a falling tree. At the autopsy they discover he had a near useless heart, and would have died soon anyway. His particular death robs him only of weeks or months, and so on the deprivation view isn't especially bad, but it is bad that he was, either way, destined to die young.

Another concern is about death's inevitability. Suppose, first, that death around 100, if not before, is in one way inevitable. We just couldn't live any longer than we do. But now just as inevitability wouldn't prevent pain from being bad — suppose everyone gets excruciating toothache in adolescence — so too with death. That fact, taken on its own, won't remove death's sting. But suppose, as seems likely, that we could live a lot longer. Imagine that at the end of this century, or the beginning of the next, scientists do find ways of improving our health, and more or less doubling our life span. We could live longer, and would do so, if this science were around now. But it isn't. Should we think that in the future, death at 80 would be seriously bad, like death at 40 now, but at present, death at 80, more or less inevitable, isn't bad at all? Think about this:

Consumptives. It's the same story throughout Victorian England. It permeates life and literature alike. Start coughing, and death, fairly soon, is more or less inevitable. You might, if you are rich, live a couple of years in a mountain sanatorium, and you just might burst forth with string of sonnets. But these are poor compensations for the loss of life. If only doctors knew then what they know now.

Develop the disease, and death is close. Yet time makes a difference. It can, now, so easily be cured. But recovery was rare, then. This doesn't, though, in any way prevent a premature death from being bad. And it's the same, arguably, with death at 100 now. Even if treatment and cures for the several conditions that carry us off are not yet available, still, if they are discovered in the future, our deaths are premature. And premature deaths are bad.

Should we agree, then, that even at 100, death is bad, and that between Diana's and Elizabeth's loss there is only a matter of degree? The argument isn't yet made. For a further issue centres on our expectations. One reason for thinking that death in old age is considerably less bad than the premature death is that people generally shape their lives with death in mind. The older we get the more it looms, we set our sights accordingly with, as time goes on, fewer plans and projects remaining unfulfilled. This fits, of course, with the modifications to the deprivation view already made above. Death is less bad, the less the periods in one's life are integrated. And, even if, should I live on, I'll find plenty to do, these plans are less well integrated if now, looking forward, it seems to me there aren't so many things to live for.

There is something of a difficulty here, however. Judy is hit by the tree as well. She's also 30, and also destined soon to die. But while James is ignorant of his heart condition she's known, for a year or more, of her fatal disease. The last few months have been given to tying up loose ends, finishing her book, deciding who'll get her CD collection, watching old Bogart films for the last time. Am I saying that, as hopes for the future drain away, so the badness of her death diminishes, and that, when the tree hits, she loses less than James? I think I am at least suggesting this, even though it remains bad that she is destined to die young, and is obliged, because of her condition, to expect from life much less than those around her.

All in all then, even if there is something bad about our having merely brief lives, it seems to me that the badness here is different in kind, and not only in degree, from the badness involved in a premature and unanticipated death. And even when anticipated, and prepared for, a death much earlier than that of your contemporaries is bad in a way that a death earlier than your successors is not.

Peaks and Troughs

Death, it seems, isn't such a mystery. It's bad when the life it deprives us of is one that would have been good for us to go on living. And, in general, the better that life, the worse it is to die. Even so, there's perhaps still something too simplistic about the picture as we so far have it. And if we think about the complexity of life, and in particular its uneven shape, its ups and downs, then we might see ways in which this account can and ought itself to be more complex. Think first about what might happen before we die. Consider:

Unjust Deserts. They're all members of the same tennis club, the veteran's team, celebrating now after a hard-earned win against challengers from up the coast. The champagne's good, and so too are the strawberries. But those oysters are contaminated. All three are in intensive care, all with less resilience than younger men, and for a while it's touch and go. They're all 60 and had, before this, another twenty years, and good years, to look forward to. But there are differences. Bill's had a good life throughout. Things came easy to him, and he's been lucky as well. A big legal practice, challenging cases, a family life that's the envy of many. Noel's had much less of this. He's been single-minded, pursuing work in medical research for near on forty years. He's on the edge now of a breakthrough, and should soon get both the recognition, and the rewards that he surely deserves. Francis, different again, has never been able to hold down much of a job. Something that happened in Korea, or that's the story. But, though he doesn't yet know it, he's got hold of a winning lottery ticket. His luck's about to change. Or it was, before the oysters.

It's a mistake, as I said earlier, to think that Bill's is the worse death because he's had, so far, the better life. All three have a lot to live for. And, if they fail to recover, they'll lose the same quality and quantity of good things in the future. But should we think their deaths are therefore equally bad? Or might we think that it's particularly bad that Noel and Francis should die now, given the upturn that their lives are about to take? Isn't it worse to lose out on the future, when it would make such a welcome contrast to the past? Hasn't Bill had more than his share of good fortune already? And is there perhaps a further distinction here? Noel's good future, if he survives, is the consequence of all his endeavours, all his sacrifices, in the past, while for Francis it's down to good luck rather than good management. Perhaps we might think, then, that of the three deaths, Noel's would be the worse.

There's a further concern about unevenness. 'Tell them I've had a wonderful life', were Wittgenstein's famous last words, but he'd been a prisoner-of-war, encountered various real and imagined setbacks with his work, had countless rows with colleagues and friends, and suffered at the end. His life might have been good overall, but it wasn't good on a day-to-day basis. So it is for all of us. And so, too, for our future lives. But perhaps this has bearing on the badness of death:

Options. Half-way across the Atlantic, and the hijackers threaten to blow up the plane. Mikhail thinks he's about to die, and judges, rightly, that if he survives, the rest of his life will be good overall. But he's going to the USA, not for a holiday, or for business, or to return home, but for a long, difficult and painful operation that cannot be carried out elsewhere. The pain will be intense, but relatively short-lived, lasting perhaps six or seven days in all. He had a similar operation once before, and though it was successful, it was agony at the time. And he's terrified by the thought of its repetition. When the hijackers strike he thinks, better to die now, suddenly, and with no pain, than to go through all that again.

Does Mikhail, in thinking this, make a mistake? It's not obvious that he does. Some people doubt that we can ever make sound judgements about the quality of life, or believe, with any real justification, that one life is better than another. But I don't doubt this. And nor do I doubt that we can make rational and irrational choices about our future lives – it's fairly clearly rational to choose, for tomorrow's dinner, chocolate ice cream over vanilla, if chocolate is your favourite. It's more complicated when different times are involved. Perhaps it's rational to prefer a short pain now, to a longer pain in the future, five minutes of the dentist's drill, to days of toothache next year. Perhaps, similarly, it's rational to put off short-term pleasures now, for longer-term pleasures in the future – forget the home cinema and think about the pension fund. Rational, perhaps, but many of us have difficulty with decisions like these. Harder still, I think, when both pleasures and pains are involved. Suppose that if you don't go to the dentist, you won't, because of sensitivity to cold, be able again to enjoy ice cream. You'll give it up, and make do with eclairs instead. So you either suffer a degree of pain tomorrow, or you get a little less pleasure for the rest of your life. Suppose you agree that if you do visit the dentist, you'll afterwards be glad that you did. Does that show you must be making a mistake if now, you decide the pain is too much to face? It doesn't seem to me clear that it does. And if it's not clear in this case, it's similarly not clear in Mikhail's case, where the pain is longer and more intense. Even supposing he knows that, if forced to accept the operation he won't, a year on, regret it, he might, I think, still be perfectly reasonable in refusing it now. So death – unending oblivion – might be preferable to pain, even if, later, compensatory pleasures will be restored.

Experience and Harm

Let's go back to something from the last chapter. What I suggested there, as a point against the Epicureans, is that even if death isn't something we experience, it does, by putting an end to everything, make a big difference to experience. It's not difficult to think that this is why it's bad. And most of the other concerns aired here have involved experience

– this is the basis for decisions by Kwame and Mikhail, if Noel's death is worse than Bill's, it's because of the different shape to their experiences, judgements about royal deaths are mostly based on experiences lost. But then what about factors that don't make a difference to experience? Can they play any part in affecting the badness of death, making one death worse than another? What we should think about here is, first, the manner of dying, and then, second, things that happen afterwards.

Does it, setting aside the different kinds of pain involved, matter how you die? Would it, for example, be worse to be murdered than to die in an accident? Intuitively it seems that it would. Think about how we respond when we hear of one child abducted and killed, and another knocked off a bicycle. Or the visceral reaction to the horror of a violent death, someone gunned down while standing at a gas station, or in some rampage at a school or hamburger joint. But there are too many complications in cases like these. We hate the perpetrator, dwell on events beforehand, forget that accidents can be violent. So imagine two people in hospital, both unconscious, both expected to recover, but both injected with fatal amounts of some drug. In Derek's case it's an accident, a nurse's blunder, while Nigel is killed by a cousin who stands to inherit his fortune. Almost certainly the cousin is worse than the nurse, but is Nigel's death worse, just because he's murdered, than Derek's?

I don't think it is. And that's in large part because I'm not sure how something can be bad for someone, or worse for that person than some other thing, if it makes no difference at all to their experience. Nigel's experience is the same, whatever the motives of his killer. So although murder is worse than negligence, it isn't clear that it brings about, for the victim at least, any greater harm.

Yet if experience is the crux, then not only is the motive of your killer irrelevant to the badness of your death, so too are the different things that might happen afterwards. There can't, in other words, be such things as post-mortem benefits or harms, so that things get better or worse for you, some time after your death. But is this right?

There's one sort of problem case here, where a deathbed promise is broken. Kafka asked his friend Max Brod to destroy his books after his death. A promise was made, but later thought better of. This was good for us, and we've got *The Trial, Metamorphosis, Amerika* and so on as a result, but there's no doubt that Brod broke his word. Yet is it in any sense bad for Kafka, is he in any way harmed, that a promise made to him hasn't been kept? It's a tricky one. Some people insist you should always keep your promises, while others say that while that's in general true, there are exceptions. And deathbed promises are included here. The first group will say, if you don't intend to keep it, don't make it. The second group reply, the important thing is to make it easier for the dying person. Say what you need to say. And so it goes on. But I think it's important to note that we might side with the first group, believing that promises should always be kept, without thinking that whenever they're broken, the person to whom the promise is made is somehow harmed.

Promising is a complicated business, and can muddy the waters. So consider a different case, where the promise is absent, but things anyway don't turn out as expected:

Children. It's not easy putting principles first. But he found he had no option, couldn't otherwise live with himself, and when the civil war came, he did all he could to help the rebels. And later, when he found himself in charge of the country, he again stinted himself. His only concern was for the good of the people, their brief lives and their immortal souls, and he died knowing that in his son's hands his life's work was safe, his plans intact. Alas, within a couple of years the monarchy was restored, his vision in tatters.

It was a lot like this for Cromwell, in England, and then again, though without the son, for Franco, in Spain. Often hopes, beliefs, a life's work are overturned by events. It happens during your life, you're aware of it, and the badness is obvious. But can your situation, your fortune deteriorate even after your death? Your reputation can suffer, your hopes can be dashed, but can any of this be bad for you? Or is it just your reputation, your hopes that are affected?

Again, I'm not sure. But I think that being dead, not existing, can't make a crucial difference. Bill and Ben together develop a successful gardening business. They're shipwrecked on Tuesday, and, though attacked by sharks, manage to fetch up on a desert island. On Wednesday Bill dies of his wounds. On Thursday their business goes bust. Never knowing of this, Ben dies on Sunday. It would be odd to draw distinctions here and insist that Ben, because he exists, is harmed by this change in fortune, while Bill, gone already, is not. Surely, whichever it is, they're in the same boat. And I'm inclined to think that neither of them suffers or is harmed by these faraway events.

One last case here. There's been a lot of concern, recently, about what happens to the body, after death. Particularly, in hospitals at Bristol and

Alder Hey the removal of organs from dead children has caused parents a lot of distress, and medical authorities a lot of embarrassment. Exhibitions of dead people, artfully displayed, skin removed, organs revealed, a sort of kitsch Vesalius, have generated not inconsiderable controversy. Controversial too, was the killing and then eating of an allegedly compliant victim in Germany. Some people pride themselves on being very matter-of-fact about such things. The person is dead. How can it matter what happens afterwards? Others are horrified at what they see as violations of the body's integrity. But how should we view such things? And this one matters a lot – there aren't going to be laws preventing deathbed promises, or post-mortem shifts in fortune, but laws about the body are necessary, important, and still up for grabs.

It's clear, first of all, that your body can be changed after your death. Indeed it will be, whether you're buried, cremated, or put on ice. It's clear, too, that it might be destroyed. And a lot of people will think it clear, as well, that it can be damaged, or harmed. And if that's right, then there's one sense in which there can be posthumous harms. But in damaging or harming your body, do I damage or harm you? That's surely less clear. Perhaps consent has something to do with it, and we can't suppose a person is harmed if her body, which she wanted cremated, is reduced to ash. But even if things don't go according to plan, and your body is handled in ways you wouldn't have wanted, it still isn't clear you're harmed.

Does this, then, vindicate the cold-hearted? No. Taboos run deep. It's interesting that only a few years before the German episode, the villain in Peter Greenaway's film, *The Cook, the Thief, His Wife and Her Lover*, finds it almost impossible to eat the body of his victim, even though it's been expertly prepared, and even though, as a villain, he's already well accustomed to the gruesome. And it may be important for all of us to treat the dead with a certain respect even while allowing that it won't be bad for them if this respect is missing. What will respect involve? In part, it's a matter of acceding to pre-mortem wishes – if you want to be cremated rather than buried, then it's probably better that you are. But in part, too, it's a matter of cultivating the appropriate response, so that in general people wish for decent things. You want your dead body to be used in some TV comedy show, or in a pornographic film, or left around for dogs to feed on. There are reasons for refusing requests like these. But we can, I think, have various complex and fine-grained reactions to the bodies of the dead without thinking that those who have died can themselves suffer any post-mortem harms.

Which Deaths Are Worse?

An idea so pervasive, long-lasting and influential as that death is the leveller isn't completely wrong. For all of us, and equally, there's annihilation, nothing further in store but ash, worms and dust. Even so, it's hard to deny that some deaths are worse than others. If we're all brought to the same level, but from different starting points, if what we lose in dying varies from case to case, then there's good reason for thinking that deaths are not all equally bad. And the deprivation view is well suited to accounting for this shifting character of death.

Even so, the deprivation view is less straightforward than at first it seems. It's not enough simply to say that the greater the quantity and quality of life lost, the worse the death, and then leave it at that. Rather, a number of further factors have to be taken into account. There's an issue about whether this future life, even if good, is better or worse than life in the past. There's the question of whether the future life is one that you expect to enjoy, or whether you've reason to think already that time is running out. And, most important, there's the matter of the connections between the life now, and the life that will be lived, if death doesn't come. For death isn't obviously bad for you if that future life will be poorly integrated into the life you have now, and so in some sense not really yours.

There are, as well, further issues to be taken into account. A number of people think that death at the end of a long life is only marginally less bad than one that comes early, just because we might, or at least might wish for, a longer life still. Well, maybe there's something in this, but even so it seems to me that any badness to death here is importantly different from badness of the more normal kind. And while usually the badness of death connects with its ending our lives, and thus ending our experience, a number of people think it can be bad, and in different cases differently bad, in ways that leave experience untouched. But the whole notion of posthumous harms – broken promises, dashed hopes, violations to the body – strikes me as suspect.

All of this matters, and matters a lot. Real-world decisions are involved. Governments in setting policy, judges in test cases and doctors in their day-to-day practice all have to come to conclusions about which lives to save. We can't believe that all lives are equally valuable, and all make an equal claim to be saved. But nor, it seems, is there an easy method to discriminate between them. We can't simply multiply quality by quantity and leave it at that. These real-world decisions have still further factors to take into account, including the costs and benefits to others of saving one life rather than another, issues relating to desert, as when ex-smokers ask for and need expensive treatment, and the effects on society as a whole of policies that might, if not properly spun, appear iniquitous. In focusing only on the badness of death for the person who dies, these further and complicating factors are side-stepped here. If, with the simpler and narrower question, we've made some progress, there's still a long way to go.

Chapter Five

Might I Live On?

When it is asked, whether Agamemnon, Thersites, Hannibal, Nero, *and every stupid clown, that ever existed in* Italy, Scythia, Bactria, *or* Guinea, *are now alive; can any man think, that a scrutiny of nature will furnish arguments to answer so strange a question in the affirmative?*
(David Hume, 'Of the Immortality of the Soul')

The Saturday magazine has a column in which celebrities are asked a string of questions about their likes and dislikes, what they think, what they worry about. One is whether they believe in life after death. About half of them do. In America, for celebrities and everyone else alike, the figure's higher, about four out of five. And these beliefs are important. Hamlet avoids killing Claudius, after confession, for fear he'll go to heaven. And heaven, and the belief they'll enter it, is usually a part of the motivation for suicide bombers. Very often, of course, it's the other place, and the horrors of hell that affect the way people behave now.

Do any such beliefs make sense? I think that mostly they do. But making sense is one thing, and being true is another. Although I think there could be an afterlife, I doubt if in fact there is.

Feeble Versions

Yet isn't it obvious that there's life after death? Some people think it is. They'll say that we live on in the thoughts of others, in the memories of our children and grandchildren, or in the minds of those who see our paintings, read our books, or benefit from sacrifices we make on their behalf. Or they'll make some appeal to science, insisting that none of us are completely destroyed by death, and that atoms, DNA, or, with transplants, perhaps even larger parts of us, will survive. And perhaps we'll live on in multiple ways. Our children remember us, preserve our photos, and they inherit our genes, our quirks.

It's true that such things happen, even if they don't happen in any significant way to all of us. A lot of people exit life, friendless, alone, and leave scarce a trace behind. A lot more are soon forgotten, their diaries unread, their family lines disappearing a couple of generations on. Of only a few can it be said, like Genghis Khan, that they have peopled a whole country, or, like Julius Caesar, that knowledge of their lives is likely to persist as long as our species survives. But even in cases like these, this handful of extremes, it just doesn't seem right to suppose these people are still alive, or that they have achieved immortality in any but a metaphorical sense. And note we wouldn't talk this way about anything else. We wouldn't say that a fresco survives so long as there remain a few fragments of painted plaster, that the Hanging Gardens of Babylon survive, because there are still some people who know what they were like, or that a giant redwood survives when its seed produces new trees, themselves to be giants in a hundred years time. For everything else, survival, living on, continuing to exist, is understood, typically, in literal terms. So why suggest anything different for people?

Part of the reason is that it can be difficult to accept that someone loved is gone, or that we ourselves will go all too soon. True or false, a belief in literal survival is often a considerable comfort. And then if such a belief becomes harder to swallow, survival in some attenuated sense can seem the next best thing. So in the Christian Church especially, and in its more sophisticated circles in particular, it's increasingly common to interpret accounts of life after death in metaphorical terms, rejecting any belief in a literal heaven or hell, a literal resurrection, and suggesting instead that we live on in the minds of others, or that we somehow remain precious in the sight of God. So rather than giving up altogether in a belief in the afterlife, these modern Christians salvage from it what they can, fashioning a slimmer but more defensible account of survival. I'm never impressed by these demythologizing moves. And I suspect that most of the celebrities in my magazine, when they talk about life after death, have a more literal meaning in mind.

There's another way the answer might be thought obvious. You're in hospital for a serious operation. While under anaesthetic your heart stops beating, perhaps only for seconds, perhaps for minutes. But the doctors manage somehow to restart it, and bring you round. So there's life after death. Yet although it's clear here that you've survived the operation, it's not at all clear, indeed it's just false, that you were brought back to life.

It's just not true that whenever someone's heart stops beating, that person dies.

Another case is harder. Some people, most of them in America, have paid a lot of money to have their bodies frozen, in the hope that at some future time scientists will be able to restore them to life. These people have probably wasted their money. For the techniques needed to make a success of cryogenics may never be perfected, and even if they are, the companies involved might well go bust in the meantime. But suppose someone is frozen, and then thawed and revived a hundred years later. Would this show that there is, after all, life after death? I have my doubts. It seems the best hope for cryogenics would be to freeze someone before they are really dead, or at the very least before their brain has started to decay. And so the best way to describe such a case is in terms of suspended animation, rather than death and resurrection. Nor does cryogenics hold out hope of a substantially longer life. So long as our bodies and brains continue to age, we'll die in the end. All it might offer, then, is a postponement of the inevitable.

Memory, inheritance, the persistence of parts, all figure in the world after death. But they are not enough, I think, to make it true that we genuinely live on. Science, and wishful thinking for science, might allow some of us to survive conditions that would otherwise be fatal. But it still seems far-fetched to suppose we can hope, by any scientific or natural means, to live again after the kinds of deaths – in road crashes, in explosions, after years of wasting disease – that many of us will suffer. Neither of these accounts seems really to hit the mark where most talk of an afterlife is concerned. What many people believe, and what is certainly profoundly important if true, are that all of us, past, present and future, will die a literal death and yet somehow live, literally, again.

Robust Versions

It's all well and good talking about literal survival, but what does that amount to? Just what is it that people believe? Different things. Many believe in life after death either with their body, or simply as a soul. Many more believe in reincarnation, where you live again but in a different body. Many, but not all of these beliefs, involve immortality – we will live again, not for weeks, years or centuries, but for ever.

The differences here are important. So we need to take these various beliefs, and separate them out.

The Body View

Here's a widespread view. Some time after death we will, in some sense, be reborn. And, the thought is, in this new life we'll have, as now, a bodily form. As St. Paul, even if not altogether clearly, puts it:

> Behold, I show you a mystery; We shall not all sleep, but we shall all be changed, in a moment, in the twinkling of an eye, at the last trump: for the trumpet shall sound, and the dead shall be raised incorruptible, and we shall be changed. For this corruptible must put on incorruption, and this mortal must put on immortality. So when this corruptible shall have put on incorruption, and this mortal shall have put on immortality, then shall be brought to pass the saying that is written, Death is swallowed up in victory. O death, where is thy sting? O grave, where is thy victory?

One important question here is about how long it will be before this resurrection takes place. A lot of Christians believe that at some time in the future, on Judgement Day, all the dead will rise again, while others believe that some sort of resurrection occurs, for each of us, fairly soon after death. This might not make that much difference to the dead – if death is nothingness, then the period between death and resurrection, however long it is, won't seem to take any time at all. But it will make a difference to those still living. For if resurrection is more or less instantaneous, then there's some hope of seeing dead people again soon. But if it's on the day of judgement, you'll have to wait.

Another question is about the shape and style of the body that is resurrected. One view is that you'll have the very same substantial, fleshy body that you've got now, while another view is that the resurrected body will be importantly different. Both views figure in Christianity, with Jesus appearing to favour the first account, while St. Paul, as in the passage above, insists that our new bodies will be significantly different from the old.

What do people believe now? Take a substantial body. Most people believe that what is supposed to have happened to Jesus was rather special – few, if any of us, are expecting a full-scale bodily resurrection a matter of days after we die. Indeed, this often seems to be something to fear, rather than to hope for. Most accounts of this sort of resurrection turn out to be horror stories – stories of vampires, zombies – infected with the thought that anyone in such a state would be neither dead nor alive but lodged, uneasily, in some intermediate state. Even when the resurrected person is less scary – and in the film *Truly, Madly, Deeply*, the Alan Rickman character, back from the dead, is, apart from being paler, just as he was in life – the general thought seems to be that it's at best inconvenient to have dead people around.

Things are different with a less substantial body. The Victorians in particular were much given to a belief in spiritualism, where the dead not only can speak to us through a medium but might be persuaded to reveal themselves in bodily form. Such bodies, though, are thin, pale, wispy – a kind of ectoplasm that seems to float around the room. The heyday of such beliefs has passed, as hopes for verifying spiritualism's claims have so often been shattered and chicanery instead so often been revealed. But a belief in ghosts continues, with many people still uneasy in an old house on a dark night.

Philosophers and the body

A lot of philosophers have found problems with orthodox resurrection accounts, where, long after death, we live again in the very same body that we inhabit now. First, it's surely going to be hard, even for God, to gather together and reassemble all our bodily parts after so many centuries have passed. But then for an omnipotent God nothing can be too hard, and we can in any event help him by ensuring, as Jews, Muslims and until recently Christians have all insisted, that our bodies are buried rather than burned, and as near as possible remain intact. But is this right? Can an omnipotent God do anything at all?

> *Cannibals.* Dr. Littlestone never expected things to be easy. As a missionary in Africa he was of course fully prepared for setbacks, trials, and tribulations. Yet he was always sustained by the certain knowledge that, whatever his fate, he would, in time, be resurrected and sit alongside his Christ. So death itself never terrified him, and the several and recurrent dangers he met in his life's work never caused his faith to waver. He had many adventures, and many escapes. But then out alone in the deepest jungle he's captured by cannibals, forced back to their village and there stewed, seasoned, and devoured.

Is there any hope, still, for his resurrection? His body isn't in some grave, mouldering but entire, ready for God or Jesus to bring back to life. Nor is it simply divided and scattered, harder but still possible to reassemble. Rather, parts of his body are now intermingled with the bodies of the cannibals. Suppose that a few days after the meal, when these parts of him have been fully digested, one of these cannibals is eaten by a tiger. It seems impossible for God to resurrect both Littlestone and the cannibal. Even God cannot put the very same atoms in two places at the same time, cannot give particular bodily parts to both the eater and the eaten on Judgement Day.

Not many of us will be eaten by cannibals, but the point here is entirely general. All of us have atoms in our bodies that were earlier in the bodies of other people when they died. Some of those atoms, in turn, were earlier in the bodies of still earlier people. And so on. God could restore, down to the very last jot, the body of any one of us. But not even God could do this for all of us.

Here's a related problem. Suppose God collects together all the atoms that were in the body of John Lennon, at the moment he was killed by Mark Chapman. He puts these atoms in the right order and, apparently, brings Lennon back to life. But God could also do the following – collect together all the atoms that were in Lennon's body at some earlier time, say when he told the audience to rattle their jewellery at the Royal Command Performance in 1963, and resurrect the younger man. All the atoms in our bodies are, naturally, exchanged over a period of time, and so God could easily make both collections. Suppose he does. Which of these people is John Lennon?

You might think the answer here is straightforward. God has to resurrect us by reconfiguring the body as it was at the time of death. And so he goes for the later Lennon. But then there's a further problem. Suppose that, like too many people, you suffer a violent death. You're burnt alive, or mangled in a car crash, or, like increasing numbers of people, you die peacefully, but at a very old age, when much of your body is no longer working or when, ravaged by disease, your mind is gone. Resurrection of this very body, as it was at the moment of death, might seem nothing to hope for. At best it appears you'd be seriously incapacitated in the life to come, while at worse, it might seem you can expect nothing but to die, more or less immediately, once again.

Are these problems real? Though some have thought they reveal serious shortcomings in the notion of resurrection, proving such a notion to be, at bottom, incoherent, something that just couldn't occur, the most they show me is that we shouldn't interpret such a notion altogether literally. Who cares about particular atoms? You can survive with much less of a body than you have now, with parts of it replaced by metal and plastic, and, at least over time, with a complete swap of the atoms that make up your body today. So surely God can do it with less than one-to-one identical parts. The cannibal problem seems to be one dreamed up by philosophers, and not any real obstacle to an afterlife. And why think God might give even a moment's thought to a double resurrection? If he did do this, then there'd be a problem in deciding which of the two is Lennon. But just because there would then be a problem, there's good reason to be confident that this is something he wouldn't do. There's reason, too, to think that an omnipotent God could remedy any physical defects, cancelling handicaps, madness, disease at a stroke and resurrecting us, if he so chooses, in our prime.

Surely, then, there aren't any serious difficulties in the idea of our being resurrected into an afterlife. We are, after all, considering something supernatural, something miraculous here, and there isn't reason to think that some picky little logic problems can really get in the way. And all this is to consider only one option, that of our living again in a body very like the one we have today. Think about the other option, a body that in some ways looks like ours, but is made instead of different, thinner, less substantial stuff. There'll be even fewer problems.

Who's Who?

Yet maybe we shouldn't be too easy-going about this. There's another problem with resurrection, and this time a big one. It's a problem about identity. For suppose we want to agree that God doesn't have to use the very same atoms that were in your body when you died – he can use different stuff. But then the question is, what makes this newly created person you? And this is surely an important question. For what many of us believe is that after death we ourselves will live again, rather than that someone else will start to exist. It matters that this new person is me, resurrected. And there's at least the beginnings of a difficulty for this idea if we allow that God can create a new person from scratch. For what's to stop this new person from being someone else?

Here are just a few suggestions. I simply make them here, and leave it, for now, at that. For this problem about identity is going to resurface later in this chapter, and then again, in Chapter 7.

- It doesn't matter what the new person is made of throughout, so long as some parts – maybe the brain, or parts of the brain – are made from the atoms that were in my body.

- It doesn't matter what the new person is made of, so long as he or she looks (more or less) like me.
- It doesn't matter what the new person is made of, or what he or she looks like, so long as he or she thinks and acts like me, and remembers what I did.

I'm not saying that any of these suggestions are especially good, though in fact I think only one of them is hopeless. They are all, though, the sorts of suggestions that might be made in connection with this identity problem.

The Soul View

A lot of people think that the afterlife is going to be very different from life as we know it now. It isn't a matter of having a perfected, or a ghostly body. Rather, what many people believe is that we'll live on, after death, with no body at all. We'll exist simply as disembodied souls.

Though this is certainly a mainstream Christian view, it doesn't seem to have been Jesus' view. It turns up in Christianity later, through contact with the Greeks, and appears in Greek thinking, in turn, from religions of the East. Socrates certainly understood and tried hard to persuade his friends and followers that after his death he'd continue to exist, just as a soul or mind, bothering other souls with his questions, no longer having to stop for lunch, to fix his toga, or even to take a night's sleep. He thought this would be good. And this idea, that the body is something we'll be better off without, is not uncommon. It needs so much care and attention, keeps going wrong, bothers us with its various appetites and demands. Let it go, release the soul and we'll be able to enjoy a purely spiritual life, a life of the mind. It's worth pointing out, though, that such a life might be better suited to philosophers and poets, than to dancers, or tennis stars, or nymphomaniacs. Their calls on the body, and what it can do, will be much less easily set aside.

So much for outlines, but there are two questions that need to be asked here. First, could there be such things as souls at all? Second, and assuming we get this far, could any of these souls be you?

The sense in souls

If the idea of souls is to make any sense at all, then there have to be things we can say about them. The first is this — a soul is going to be some sort of spiritual thing, something non-material, non-physical. And, second, a soul is some sort of thinking thing, a thing with a mind, or a mental existence.

Are there any non-physical things? Or is everything in the universe made of physical stuff? It's a mistake to think that physical things are always solid, and always visible. Clouds are physical things, as are genes and radio waves. Other things, chess problems, poems, numbers, are non-physical through and through. But souls are different. They're neither thinly physical, like X-rays, nor abstract, like recipes. So it's looking like souls would have to be some very special kind of non-physical thing.

But a lot of people will object. They'll say we're already well aware of a whole host of soul-like items, particular things that are both non physical and thinking. Just consider our own minds. They're close to, and connected with brains and bodies, perhaps, but they're entities of a different kind. Descartes, especially, is known for his insistence that we can tell, just by thinking clearly and distinctly about it, that minds are one thing, one kind of thing, and bodies are another. And it's the mind that matters. We are, essentially, minds or thinking things, that just happen to be lodged inside bodies, rather as – his analogy – a captain might be inside his ship. But then a lot of people have argued that it isn't as clear as Descartes would have it. Though it's pretty obvious there are bodies without minds – stones, tables, oak trees – it's not yet obvious that there are, or can be, minds without bodies. Nor is it obvious that we, now, are a mix of the two separate things. Maybe our minds are a bit like radio programmes: there are thoughts, beliefs, memories, and these aren't simply bits of stuff, but they wouldn't be there at all, they wouldn't exist, if there weren't bits of stuff – bodies, brains, nerve endings, electrical impulses – all working together in particular ways, and giving rise to beliefs, memories, desires and the like. And surely it would be odd if this weren't true, odd if the correspondences between thoughts, on the one hand, and brain behaviour, on the other, weren't at all necessary, and were just a series of coincidences, arbitrary, a fluke, and down to chance.

Some philosophers have built upon these doubts about dualism – Descartes' idea that there are two different kinds of stuff – and suggested that souls make no sense. For if minds depend on brains, there just couldn't be any sort of disembodied mind. But it doesn't seem to me obvious that there couldn't be souls. It's one thing to find holes in arguments that try to prove that our minds and bodies are separate things, and quite another to show that the idea of a disembodied mind is altogether incoherent. After all, if it were incoherent, if even God couldn't create souls, it would seem that God himself couldn't exist. For he too is supposed to be a non-physical yet thinking thing, and therefore is himself a kind of soul.

There are, though, further problems with the soul view. On most accounts of the afterlife, souls don't simply think — they recognise and communicate with one another. But could disembodied souls really have a social life? Right now we engage, usually, with other people by first moving into a space close to theirs, and then each of us using bits of our body — eyes, hands, mouths — to communicate with the other. Souls won't be able to do this. Nor will they, instead, be able simply to will themselves into another's mind. For genuine communication includes the option of saying no. You want to talk to Marilyn Monroe, but she's busy, again, with Einstein.

Again, though, it seems the problems here might be exaggerated. Souls could seem to see each other, seem to move around in space, seem to talk. And maybe they could communicate by a kind of telepathy, infecting one another's thoughts sometimes successfully, sometimes, as when the other soul is busy, leaving a disembodied text message. We can leave for now how interesting such a life would be, especially if it goes on for a long time, but nevertheless it does seem as if it might be possible.

Could a soul be me?

I said that there would be further occasions when we'd need to consider identity problems in this chapter. And there are two such problems that come up now. For it's not enough, where belief in the afterlife is concerned, to be persuaded that there could be disembodied souls, things that, while only mental, might in some important ways be like persons. We need to be persuaded, also, that each of us could be one of these souls. But can we be persuaded of that?

The first problem emerges from a point about dualism. Suppose we agree that we are not, at present, some kind of mix of two distinct things — a physical body and a non-physical mind or soul. Does this put an end to the soul view? Could you, in other words, become a soul, if you are not one now? I don't see why not. Many things can survive a change in the material in which they are embedded — a piece of music can be written down or played by an orchestra, a poem might be etched on a printer's plate, kept in electronic form on a computer's hard drive, or simply memorized. What matters, in these cases, is that what strikes us as important is present in both versions, and that the one is the cause of the other. And if we think the important thing about a person is their mind – their personality, character, memory, and so on – and we think that such things might exist in a non-material form, then, surely, a person might survive this change in substance, existing first as a physical, later as a spiritual, being.

The second problem connects with those suggestions made above, about how to manage difficulties in bodily resurrection. How could we be persuaded that the reborn person is you? Neither looking like you, nor thinking like you, nor both together is enough. Nor will it clinch things if, on top of this, the new person believes she is you. Consider an ordinary case:

> *Too Identical Twins?* They have a lot in common – looks, the way they move, a taste in clothes. But still, Carol and Susan, although identical twins, are different people. Both are up for it at the wedding party, when the hypnotist asks for volunteers. He can hardly believe his luck, the twist it will give his act, when the twins step forward. He puts Carol in a trance first, tells her she's Susan, and asks her questions – for some of those present, way too many – about her past.

Whatever she does, whatever she looks like, and whatever she believes, Carol isn't Susan. That much is surely clear. But it's clear too that this case is different from those concerning the afterlife. First, one reason for insisting that Carol isn't Susan is that Susan herself is still around, making a much stronger claim. Second, we can put our finger on the trickery in this case, and so can confidently say, for example, that Carol only *seems* to remember what Susan did. Third, we can assume here that the resemblances are both partial and temporary – there's much in Susan's life that Carol doesn't even seem to remember and, if the hypnotist is not to be sued, the differences between the sisters will soon be restored. But the story with souls is different in all three respects: the soul appears after you die, we've no reason to suppose there's any trickery involved, and the replication of your mental life is thorough and persistent. I'm not saying that this proves the soul *is* you, but only that many of the more obvious grounds for suspicion are thereby removed. Again, we can take this further in the later chapter.

One final point here. These problems emerge only on the assumption that we are not already souls, with our bodies as temporary shelters. But if I am a soul now, any soul in the afterlife will be me just in case it's the same soul. And those problems that threatened resurrection views just won't surface here. For souls, unlike bodies, presumably remain intact throughout, and don't involve parts to which others might lay claim.

The Reincarnation View

Another view about the afterlife appears in important ways to combine aspects of the two accounts above. Believers in reincarnation think that after death we will be reborn, yet with a different body. Perhaps you'll return as someone else, perhaps as an animal, or a bird, or an insect. Having a body is important, then, but we can live on without any particular body, or even any particular kind of body. So just what is it that makes this other person, or animal me? It's me because it contains my essence, or spirit, or soul.

Reincarnation views, even though they're growing in popularity worldwide, are most often associated with the major religions of the East – Hinduism, Buddhism, and Sikhism. These religions have a fair amount in common, as do the so-called religions of the book – Judaism, Christianity and Islam. And the differences between their accounts of the afterlife, with reincarnation, on the one hand, and – most typically – resurrection, on the other, are profound.

First, and most obvious, because believers in reincarnation see us as essentially non-material things – minds, or spirits or souls – they have no interest in preserving the body after death. Hence the marked contrast, tempered only recently, between Western burial and Eastern cremation.

A more important difference is that reincarnation typically involves an altogether depersonalized account of what life after death consists in. Even if you were once an Aztec warrior, and will in the future return as a goat, you can't hope to remember anything of this previous existence, or expect that the goat will either remember your life today, or have about it anything of your character or personality. Suppose you're an extrovert, crazy about dancing, and with a good sense of humour. The goat is unlikely to exhibit such traits. And we are wrong about Hindus, Buddhists and Sikhs if we suppose they think that some goats have a goat mind while others think of themselves as human beings trapped in a goat's body. Something like this is what happens to the frog prince in the fairy tale, but it isn't what happens to us, in the Eastern religions. And so while such religions share with some versions of Christianity a belief in souls, these souls are understood in very different ways.

Even so, the goat's lot is not altogether separate from yours. Central to most accounts of reincarnation is the idea of karma, the idea that responsibility for actions in one life is carried forward into the next. If you're a wicked person, the goat will have a lot to answer for. And related to this is the idea that there are no unexplained evils. What may appear to us an unfortunate accident, say, that your children are blind from birth, or that your cousin loses everything in a stock market crash, will be seen as a punishment for the sins of an earlier life.

Further differences, hinted at in what has already been said, concern the desirability and the extent of the afterlife. Though reincarnation goes on and on, and on Hindu accounts is going to occur 84 million times, the cycle of death and rebirth is not endless. Nor is this a bad thing. The closer we are to quitting this cycle, to a complete shedding of the self, to nirvana, the better it is. In stark contrast to the major monotheisms, then, believers in reincarnation hold non-existence as an ideal.

Could I be reincarnated?

There's room for argument about parts of this, and no doubt some people will think that my sketch in places distorts or oversimplifies what reincarnation is to involve. Perhaps. Eastern religions, unlike those from further West, have never been altogether systematized and codified, and it is hardly surprising that many of their followers see things in different ways. Even so, many of these followers themselves agree that there is a deep difficulty at the core of reincarnation accounts, a difficulty in understanding just how it can claim to be an account of life after death.

Just what is it that is supposed to live on? If neither my body, nor my mind – memories, beliefs, personality, character – survive my death, why should I think there's any chance that I will be reborn? Believers in reincarnation have an answer here. They insist that it's the soul, or spirit, or essence that survives, and because this survives, we will live again. But this answer is thin as it stands, and unless it can be unpacked, nothing much is gained.

Just suppose there is within all of us, and within animals and maybe plants as well, some kind of spiritual stuff, something non-physical that survives our bodily death and resurfaces elsewhere, in another form. So what? Bits of physical stuff can travel from one body to another, but that won't in itself bring about my survival. Why should a similar migration of spiritual stuff be any more important, unless that spiritual stuff is me? And as it's not enough simply to say that an atom or lump of bone, or heart, is me, so it's not enough just to say the spiritual stuff is a soul, and then to say the soul is me. Life after death surely demands more than this. Consider:

> *Peter, Paul and Mary.* After years together on the road, moving from town to town, singing, playing guitars, both Peter and Paul die and are cremated. Peter is reincarnated, and returns to this life as a swallow. Paul ceases to exist completely, but soon after his death a swallow is born. Mary, their younger sister, lives on alone in their partially converted barn. And, always a spiritual person herself, she learns of their different fates in a dream. Come the spring, and the swallows nest in her barn. She wonders which of the two is Peter, but has to admit she can't see any significant difference between them. She has to admit, too, that she can't really imagine what the significant difference would be. Swallows is swallows . . .

There are two points here. It might be hard to tell two things apart, even though the things are importantly different. A doctor might be unable to discover which of two people is nurturing some fatal disease. Even so, he knows what the difference is, why it matters and how, in time, it will show up. But it's not simply that Mary can't herself decide which of these birds is her brother, and which is merely a bird. She can't even make proper sense of the idea that one of them might be Peter. She has no difficulty with the idea that one might contains bits of Peter, either mental bits of physical bits. But that doesn't seem to help. Nor is she helped by notions of the transfer of responsibility from one life to the next. Suppose Peter was for years a vicious brute, and one of the birds is always sick. Mary might be persuaded that one is the cause of the other. But until she's persuaded that the swallow is Peter, this strikes her as a profound injustice, rather than well-deserved retribution. So far as she can make out, then, there's no important difference, now, between Peter and Paul. There's no important difference between death and reincarnation, on the one hand, and death followed by a separate birth, on the other.

Mary's worries are, of course, mine. A soul that carries with it no beliefs, no memories, no character from one life to the next is, it seems, a soul in name only. If it is in this way stripped of all psychological features, this so-called soul, whatever it is, cannot be me. As far as I can tell, then, reincarnation views, even if they involve the near-endless recycling of something or other, don't in any thoroughgoing way constitute a worthwhile account of a life after death.

Is There an Afterlife?

What I've suggested is that on two of the three views above, life after death is at least possible. It doesn't seem to me to be incoherent or illogical to suggest that there might, after my death, be someone alive who, first, is in some important ways like me, and who, second, really is me, the very same person. Maybe in this new life I have some sort of body, or maybe I exist just as a soul. Both suggestions seem to me to make sense.

But to agree that there is this bare possibility of survival isn't of course, yet to agree that any of us will survive. Lots of things are possible – winning the lottery every week for a year, being hit by a meteorite just when you say 'meteorite', neighbours who, every time you're out, break in to your house, hold wild parties, then clean up the mess and disappear – but there is no reason to believe such things actually happen. Is it the same with the afterlife? Is this just a wild fancy, or do we have reason to think it might occur?

Could there be evidence?

Here's a story about life after death:

> *The Power of Prayer.* Their princess is killed, and the people are stricken with grief. So much of what they'd hoped for was invested in her, so strongly did they believe her when she said she'd be their Queen of Hearts. There are remembrance services throughout the land, and, for the funeral, a national day of mourning. She is buried, like King Arthur, on an island. And then, surely it's a miracle, she returns to us. At first the stories are met with suspicion – it's a joke, it's the drink, it's an impostor. But there she is, the very same woman. When, still suspicious, they open the coffin, there's nothing there.

This would be a kind of miracle. And some of us would refuse to believe it. But should we? That enemy of religion, David Hume, seems to have argued that we could never have reason to believe that such a thing ever happens. There are so many other explanations – hallucinations, trickery, the fact that people are gullible – with each of them more likely to be behind any so-called miracle than genuinely supernatural events. After all, miracles, almost by definition, are supposed to be extraordinary, to be at utterly at odds with our everyday experience. We ought always to be suspicious. Still, it seems to me that there could come a time when this appeal to ordinary explanations is exhausted, and there's no reasonable option but to accept that the extraordinary, even the miraculous, has occurred. Or take another kind of case, less fantastic:

> *The Séance.* You wouldn't really notice her in the street, or pick her out from her friends in The Star and Garter. Most of the time there's nothing especially special about Beryl. Until she goes into her trance. She's been interested in spiritualism for years, ever since an uncle died and his daughter, her cousin, started to go to meetings. Then, later, Beryl found she could make contact with those on the other side. Last Thursday for example, in her trance, in a sort of swooning, and then, in a different, a gravelly voice, she seemed to become the mouthpiece for a man who said his name was Jeb, and had fought against Boney's lot, off the coast off Spain.

What should we say about this sort of thing? Of course, there's usually a natural explanation, conning or self-deception, or a kind of hysteria. And the stories from 'the other side' are usually commonplace, stuff anyone could learn from books, or make up. But we can at least imagine a case that involves claims about events that no one now could possibly know, where all this is carefully noted, where there are plenty of reliable witnesses, and where later discoveries prove these claims to be true. Even so, this still might be no more than an amazing coincidence. But if we think there could be souls, and that they could somehow communicate with us, then, it seems to me, we have to allow that there could be evidence, even if never conclusive evidence, to suggest that it is indeed a soul that we've encountered. And, in a case like this, it seems the right sort of evidence might have been amassed.

Is there evidence?

This is still fantasy land. To say there could be evidence is not yet to say that such evidence has ever been found. And I think the biggest obstacle to believing in life after death is just this, that at the end of the day the evidence is never particularly strong. Perhaps Jesus did rise from the cross, after three days, and walk and talk with his disciples, but there's just no good reason to believe that he did. Perhaps there are vampires, but there is as yet no reason to believe in them. Perhaps we live on as souls, and might, after death, make our peace with our enemies, express regret for all the things left unsaid, or said in haste, and live a life of contemplation. But again, there is no reason to believe any such thing.

My scepticism here will be accepted by many who do believe in such things. For what many religious people insist on is that it's faith, rather than reason, that sits behind their key beliefs. Others, though, will want to say that there are many cases where the evidence is strong. And in recent years so-called near-death experiences, reported by 1 in 20 Americans, have been a widely discussed as providing evidence of an afterlife. This is hard to understand. Being near death, after all, is importantly different from being dead. Indeed, it could be said that all of us are fairly near to death, all of the time. And there are much simpler explanation as to why someone might, after an operation in which, say, their heart stopped beating for a while, report that it seemed to them they saw a welcoming stranger in a bright light at the end of a tunnel, or that they could see themselves, as if from above, on the operating table. None of these people were ever really dead. And of course if they had been, we'd then have excellent evidence for life after death, though brought about by doctors rather than God, whatever it was they remembered.

It would be a mistake, however, to think that such experiences are a recent phenomenon. Bede, writing in eighth-century England, tells the story of man who apparently died in the middle of the night, only to come back to life the next morning. This man describes what happened to him:

> A handsome man in a shining robe was my guide, and we walked in silence in what appeared a north-easterly direction . . . He soon brought me out of darkness into an atmosphere of clear light, and as he led me forward in bright light, I saw before us a tremendous wall which seemed to be of infinite length and height in all directions. As I could see no gate, window or entrance in it, I began to wonder why we went up to the wall. But when we reached it, all at once — I know not by what means — we were on top of it. Within lay a very broad and pleasant meadow . . . Such was the light flooding all this place that it seemed greater than the brightness of daylight or of the sun's rays at noon.

Little changes. And again, the right reaction, I'd suggest, is to take all this with a pinch of salt.

Might I Live On?

What's the answer? I've wanted to suggest, in contrast to the arguments of several philosophers, that some forms of afterlife are possible. We might live again in one or other bodily form, or we might exist just as disembodied souls. Might we, instead be reincarnated? I've expressed doubts. But this isn't because I think it impossible that something should migrate from one body to the next. Rather, it's because, on the reincarnation believer's own account of what this thing is, it's hard to see how this promises an afterlife for me.

Is it important that I disagree with those who are sceptical about a possible afterlife? To a degree, but this disagreement is more about what philosophy can achieve than it is about what, after death, is in store for us. For, as I've indicated, I am sceptical in turn, sceptical of attempts to altogether rule out, by reason and argument, the bare possibility of life after death.

And what can we do with this bare possibility? Not a lot. There's a world of difference between allowing that survival is possible and arriving at a position where an afterlife seems certain or even probable. And, though many will disagree strongly, I want to suggest there is just no good reason, no strong evidence, to think that any of us will live on.

Chapter Six

Should I Take the Elixir of Life?

. . . the people who ask for death earliest are a bit like you. People who want an eternity of sex, beer, drugs, fast cars — that sort of thing. They can't believe their good luck at first, and then, a few hundred years later, they can't believe their bad luck.

(Julian Barnes, *A History of the World in 10½ Chapters*)

Many will. Given half a chance of immortality, they'll grab at it. This is hardly surprising. If death is, as it appears to be, a bad thing, then surely it's best avoided for as long as possible. And best of all if it can be avoided completely, so that we can live on forever. Even if we doubt they'll ever succeed, the idea that scientists might one day do away with death is, it seems, something we all could hope for. And even if there are corresponding doubts about heaven, this similarly, is something we might well want to pray for. So an elixir, a magic formula, a pathway to eternity is, even though the stuff of fantasy, a welcome fantasy neverthe-less. And, just suppose it should come your way, you'd surely want to take it.

Yet not so fast. Life can be bad, and death can sometimes be better. And if nothingness can be preferable to earthly troubles, it can surely be better by far than the fires, the pitchforks, the unspeakable torments of hell. Read Dante, look at Bosch, and any naïve enthusiasm for the afterlife will very soon be checked. Better nothing at all than an existence like this. And better, if needs must, a week in hell than to be there for all eternity. So we need to consider carefully the situation we might be getting ourselves into. Not all versions of an immortal life should figure on our wish list.

The suggestions made here, uncontroversially, are that an immortal life wouldn't necessarily be good. It depends, surely, on the kind of life on offer. But then several people have wanted to suggest as well that immortality would necessarily not be good. So whatever the elixir promises, we'd be mad to take it. This is controversial. I'm not altogether sure that this controversial claim is true. But it's worth thinking about.

Variant Lives

Immortality could take on many forms. You'd be unwise to accept any potion, commit to any unending life, until you've looked through the fine print, made certain exactly what's on offer, and discovered just what the costs, to you and to others, might be. Some of the problems, such as hell, will be obvious. Others might be harder to spot. So it all needs more detail.

There's a big distinction, first of all, between, on the one hand, the sorts of afterlife promised or threatened by different religions – an afterlife of the supernatural kind – and then, on the other, the hope, at least, of immortality here on earth. Think about the first. While hell might obviously be bad, it shouldn't simply be assumed that heaven, of any traditional kind, will be that much better. Don't forget, immortality is forever, and forever might seem a long time to play the harp, to contemplate the eternal verities, or to praise God. The vision of heaven given in the Koran is richer in detail, and will no doubt appeal to many:

> The true servants of Allah will be well provided for, feasting on fruit, and honoured in the gardens of delight. Reclining face to face on soft couches, they shall be served with a goblet filled at a gushing fountain, white, and delicious to those who drink it. It will neither dull their senses nor befuddle them. They shall sit with bashful dark-eyed virgins, as chaste as the sheltered eggs of ostriches.

But again, a couple of weeks of this might be better than all eternity.

Think, instead, about an endless continuation of life on earth, and there's even more to watch out for. You'd be well advised, before taking any elixir, to find out whether it merely stops you from dying, or whether it arrests ageing as well. The Struldbuggs, in *Gulliver's Travels*, have immortal lives, but of a distinctly unattractive kind:

> At ninety they lose their teeth and hair; they have at that age no distinction of taste, but eat and drink whatever they can get, without relish or appetite. The diseases they were subject to still continue without increasing or diminishing. In talking, they forget the common appellation

of things, and the names of persons, even of those who are their nearest friends and relations. For the same reason, they never can amuse themselves with reading, because their memory will not serve to carry them from the beginning of a sentence to the end; and by this defect they are deprived of the only entertainment whereof they might otherwise be capable . . .

And they are, so far, only 90. It gets worse. Gulliver's somewhat understated comment is that, in light of this, his 'keen appetite for perpetuity of life was much abated'.

But what if you're old already? Or an adolescent, gawky, with spots? Many of us would prefer to choose some ideal age, first adding or dropping a decade or two, and then sticking at it, or at least appear to stick at it, forever. Some, though, have worried that this might not be as good as it first seems: 'To be thirty-five for two years sounds attractive, certainly. But for three years? A little dull, surely. For five years – ridiculous. For ten – tragic.' Others see no problem here and, having settled on their prime, would be happy to continue there.

It's not only, though, disease and ageing that you'll need to be concerned about. What would be the point of living forever if, like the rest of us, you could lose an arm to a crocodile, and then a leg in a skiing accident, or be shot through, or decapitated? And then if you fell into a vat of acid, or were blown to pieces in some war, surely there'd be nothing for it but to die? It's around here that realistic hopes for the immortal life come under pressure – even if they can bring an end to ordinary signs of ageing, even if they can eliminate, or always counter disease, scientists are unlikely to find ways of guaranteeing that we'll be able to stay alive whatever the circumstances. Just as a painting might last indefinitely, given proper care, but might as well, if it's neglected, be destroyed, so too for human lives under any realistic and non-supernatural account.

So forget realism for now. An elixir is fantastic already, so let's just add to the fantasy, and imagine that if you take it, you will live forever, no matter what. And let's add as well, that you'll live in a good condition – holes will disappear, parts will re-grow. Don't worry about the details of how.

A different sort of question concerns the relation to others. An elixir might be offered to you alone, or it might, rather like fluoride, be put into the water supply. Or perhaps, as a compromise, you'll be able to nominate a dozen or so fellow immortals, and so be able to share forever with those closest to you. The options here will make a big difference. Not to age, not to die, while those around you remain subject to the bruises of time might at first appeal to the vain among us, but is likely in the longer run to be alienating, setting you too far apart from others, and making the fleeting nature of relationships — you live on, they die — altogether inescapable. And you'll need either to be a deceiver, vanishing and then taking on a new identity every few years or, if you let the secret out, prepared to be treated as a freak by everyone you meet. Better, then, perhaps, for this to be a common fate, with the shape and pattern of your life very much reflected in those around you.

The Best Life

People are unlikely to agree about these different versions of immortality. Some of us want to be rid of the body, and to spend a more or less unchanging eternity with God, Christ and the angels. Others enjoy their present lives, and would be happy for them to continue forever. Of those, some would like a lot of company, while others prefer to be special. Almost no one wants hell.

Some versions of an eternal life would be bad. Others might be alright, but not your first choice. But can it be true, as some suggestions have it, that there is just no detailed account of immortality that ought to tempt us? Can it be true that even if you're given a free hand to sort out the fine print as and how you choose, you ought still, if you've got any sense, to decline the offer, and leave the elixir where it is, untouched? Can it be right to decide, in the end, that it's better to die than endlessly to live on?

Think about the different ways in which you might be immortal. Choose whichever you think the best of these. Imagine an elixir that, if you take it, will guarantee for you this life. One important reminder — immortality is forever; the offer is not for a life just as long as you choose it to be. The offer is made: a once in a lifetime chance to become immortal. Would you accept?

An Immortal Life

The Emperor wants eternal life, and has his alchemists in Prague working towards a formula. Eventually one of them, Hieronymous Makropulos, comes up with something that promises with each dose to extend life by 300 years. But he's made to test it first on his daughter. She reacts badly, falls ill, and though she recovers, the Emperor is understandably reluctant to take it himself. And of course he's no idea that the elixir does in fact work.

All this is in the background to Janáček's opera, *The Makropulos Case*. It's the present, and Elina Makropulos, seemingly young and beautiful, is now 337 years old. She's a singer, wealthy, fascinating to men and women alike, but with something disturbing, something of the night about her. Strings of affairs and classrooms full of children all abandoned, she's had to reinvent and rebrand herself a number of times, disappearing whenever her apparent youth starts to raise suspicions. She's always stuck with the same initials, though – Elian MacGregor, Eugenia Montez, Ekaterina Myshkin – and when the work opens she's presenting herself as Emilia Marty, back in Prague where it all began, and on the hunt for the formula, which she somehow managed to lose centuries ago. But though she finds it in time, she begins to realize that the endless life is no longer what she wants:

> Life should not last so long! If you only realised how easy it is for you. You are so close to everything. For you, everything makes sense. For you everything has value. Fools, you are blissful, for the trivial chance reason that you are going to die so soon. But in me life has come to a halt, Christ, and can go no further! What hideous solitude! It's all in vain, Krista, whether you sing or keep silent – no pleasure in being good, no pleasure in being bad. No pleasure on earth, no pleasure in heaven. And one comes to learn that the soul has died inside one.

And so she dies, and the formula is destroyed.

Is this feeble of her? Is it a story about a personal tragedy, an individual failure of nerve, or is it, instead, and as many operas claim to be, about the human condition, the point being made that any of us would in the end want out? It's been seen that way. And the philosopher Bernard Williams has argued that EM, as he calls her, makes the only rational decision open to her, and that we'd all, sooner or later, choose death to yet more of life. Others, though, while impressed with the strength of his conviction, think that Williams simply betrays his own attitude to life in taking EM's side: some people will want to call it day, but others will be dying to go on.

Just what are the problems with immortality? Why is it, allegedly, in the end so unattractive? We can, following Williams, mention three.

Does anyone really want to visit all the beaches in Africa? Or follow *The Simpsons* for as long as possible? Or to read every book ever written? I remember when I was a student and getting excited about a production of *Hamlet* at the local theatre. I couldn't understand it when the woman who taught us Italian – she was around 60 at the time – said she'd seen *Hamlet* often enough, and didn't much care to see it again. But in fact it's true that for many of us, there does come a time when going to Barcelona, eating oysters, seeing the fireworks at New Year just isn't as exciting as once it was. There does come a time when, whatever it is we're doing, if we keep at it, we start to get bored.

A lot of people will disagree with this, and imagine that boredom will never set it. They're almost certainly wrong. But even those who agree will object that although we might get bored with one thing, we can always move on to something else. After all, there's really a lot of stuff out there in the world, and not only will it take centuries, if not quite forever, to scratch its surface, it's true also that it keeps getting added to – people write more books, make more films, send more space probes to more distant planets. So maybe it's just wrong to think we'd ever run out of things to do, wrong to think there'd be a time when we couldn't develop new interests, and wrong to think that boredom might in any sense be inevitable.

There are a number of things to say about this. Some of it is said below. But one point to bring up now concerns the link between boredom and the question of whether your immortal life is to be shared, or solitary. Suppose, like EM, that immortality makes you special. Others die. It's surely very likely that, at least until they make themselves extinct, these mortals will keep up the flow of new things for you to get interested in. New people will be born, get excited about *Hamlet*, and put on yet more dreary student productions. There'll be new ideas for things to do with food, a degree of variation in Abba tribute bands, breakthroughs in reality TV. At least a trickle, then, of novelty. But suppose instead that everyone is immortal. The chances of boredom seem to be substantially increased. For first, there are no new people coming along, bringing with them new ideas. And second, and related, the existing people are surely likely, sooner or later, to stultify, running out steam, and finding almost nothing a stimulus to innovation. Before too long, from infinity's perspective, you might all have written and read all the novels you can take. A world of immortals, then, is a world very much lacking the incentive and motivation to change.

Depth

A different, though connected, concern is about the inevitable lack of seriousness and depth in an immortal life. Think about our present lives, in all their stages, and it's going to be clear that a lot of what matters most to us, a lot of life's rewards and frustrations, concern those choices that once made, cannot easily be undone, and, once made, rule out a host of other choices. So it matters a lot which subjects we take at school, what to do about a career, who we might marry, when, if at all, to have children, whether to stick it out in this country, or sell up and try our hand elsewhere. Get these things wrong, and there can be a lifetime of regret. Maybe it matters a lot too that we walk the Appalachians while still up to it, see Baryshnikov during rather than after his prime, that we settle things with relatives before they die. The point here isn't just that our lives overall are relatively short, but that they are short too in each of their stages, and in each of those stages decisions are made, often irreversible, that then narrow down opportunities elsewhere. I long ago gave up all hope of being a ballet dancer, and becoming even moderately good at darts or snooker is looking more and more like a long shot. And it's this critical patterning and funnelling to our inevitably brief lives that invests them with their seriousness, importance, and weight.

All this changes when what's on offer is immortality. It's not just getting a second chance, time to rethink, to pursue a different career, to try again with the family thing. Rather it's to have an infinity of such chances. But then why agonize over a decision when it's a matter not of now or never, but of sooner or later? If you'll live forever, and under your best conditions, you can be a rock star, a tennis champion, and prime minister to boot, even if not all at the same time. And why try, making every effort to pass some test, prepare for and land a job, climb a mountain, if there's always tomorrow? Of course, there are some things we care about even if it's not now or never – I'm hoping to win this squash game tonight even though there are plenty more games to come. But in other cases it really is part of being up against the clock that invests what we do with urgency and importance. And with the immortal life this need for awareness of time is mostly gone. Mostly, for if others are still mortal, and it's one of them you want, then you'll need to go for it.

But then why lose sleep over the one, when there'll be others just as good coming along?

Some people are likely to accept a part, but only a part of this. They'll agree that it does matter, and often matters terribly, when we get things wrong. And given forever, and a superfluity of chance, the pains of regret will be much reduced. But surely there can't be anything wrong with that? Avoiding pain is good. And it doesn't at all follow from this that the satisfactions of getting them right are reduced. For there's an interesting difference here. When thing go wrong, we think of what might have been. When they go right, we're focused, typically, on the here and now. You're scoring goals for Arsenal, dating the person you want to date, winning an election, watching a soufflé rise. And if it's the here and now, it's the same whether there's forever ahead of you, or just a few more years.

Yet there are reasons to doubt whether, beyond a handful of cases, human beings are ever fully absorbed just in the present. It might be like this while the dentist is drilling into your tooth, or in the middle of a rally in tennis, but for most of us, for most of the time, focus is never more than partial. Think of a piece of music, say a symphony by Mozart. You can't be listening to the development section properly unless you're aware of just which themes, now only in the memory, are being developed. Second, as this example makes clear, it's not simply a matter of looking ahead but often, looking back as well. And where immortality is concerned there's plenty of opportunity for that. But then how much can it matter, how satisfying can it be to score goals for Arsenal when you know you've been doing that for a century or so already? Or take the more important, and considerably more familiar case of falling in love. Some people believe this is a once in a lifetime thing, while others might need fingers and thumbs to count the times it's happened to them. But could anyone fall in love a hundred times, thinking, yet again, that they've never felt this way before, that this is it, that the earth moved? If you can fall in love that often, then perhaps you can't really fall in love at all.

The concern, then, is that it's in very large part the pressures of time that give shape and meaning to our lives. Remove those pressures and we're in danger of drifting on, endlessly, gesturing at importance and value, but achieving none. Something like this is Faustus' predicament, in the middle scenes of Marlowe's play. Having sold his soul to the devil in return for limitless power, Faustus wastes his life on a series of conjuring tricks, teasing the pope and his cardinals, devising dumb shows for the emperor, morphing his enemies into beasts. It's as if when, because we've either unlimited power, or unlimited time, we can do anything, we find there's no longer anything that we really want to do.

Character

There's a further problem here. For to go back to the point about boredom. Are you really someone who, if time permits, can get interested in just about anything? Or are you instead someone who, more or less, knows what they like? I know that although I'm still interested in new things, there's a lot that's just not and never will be for me. I'm never going to get excited about golf, or manga cartoons, or holidays on the beach. They're not my thing. And this doesn't, I hope, make me some kind of stick in the mud, someone not at all open to new ideas or influences. It does, though, connect with my being by this stage of my life settled in certain ways, a person with certain sorts of interests, and concern, a person with a certain sort of character.

Something like this is certainly an issue for EM. It isn't simply that she is growing old, unaccountably tired with and bored by the new experiences that seem always to be on offer. It's rather that she has grown up, and that it is no longer psychologically possible for her to have the open-ended zest for the new that is appropriate to youth. As Williams puts it, she suffers 'a boredom connected with the fact that everything that could happen and make sense to one particular human being of 42 had already happened to her. Or rather, all the sorts of things that could make sense to one woman of a certain character . . .'. And the point, of course, is that this fixing of character, and its consequent limiting of future experience, is not at all something we should regret, or wish we were without. Rather, to take life and what it has to offer seriously, to give it the attention it deserves, and the attention you probably need to give it, if you're going to get much out of it, just will involve you in cutting down on your options. A life that doesn't shape you, doesn't leave its mark is, most likely, a life only half-lived.

A Human Life

The overall suggestion, then, is that there seems in the end to be a deep and stubborn incompatibility between the idea of an endless life on the one hand, and our understanding of human existence, on the other. First thoughts about immortality suggest that it can offer us just more, and a welcome more, of the life we already lead. But it's beginning to seem that this isn't so, and that an immortal life would be so deeply different from the life we know that it's hardly something we could want for ourselves.

This, though, is vague. And it isn't yet clear enough whether we should think, as Williams seems to think, that an immortal life would in the end be worse than any alternative, or whether instead, it would merely be very different from, and much worse than, a good life of the familiar and mortal kind. If the former, then taking the elixir would always be irrational, whereas if it's the latter, it will depend on the alternative life on offer. So consider:

> *Drinkers.* Sammy and Rosie are in their favourite bar, chatting, listening to music, enjoying a couple of drinks. It's Hallowe'en, so they're not at first surprised when they're approached by a mysterious stranger, head to toe in black, his face half-covered, his voice suspiciously low. He offers them yet another drink, telling them and – though heaven knows how – persuading them that it's the elixir of life. After thinking about it, and texting friends for advice, they both accept. Is this odd? Perhaps. But there's an important difference between them. Though they're both now 30, Sammy is a picture of health, a success at work, madly in love with Alice, just starting his first novel. Rosie is seriously ill, and knows she'll be lucky to see in the New Year.

Sammy's living the good life, and can expect it to continue for maybe another fifty years. Perhaps he's made a mistake here, crazy to swap this for a life without end, given the disadvantages that Williams describes. But what about Rosie? For her, and very soon, it's immortality or death. It's a question of which is worse.

If the points made above are correct, then she can expect, if she takes the elixir, to find much in life less interesting than it was. At the least, she'll often be bored. She can expect too, to find her life in many ways trivial and shallow. And the more she retains her character, the more she remains herself, the more this boredom and triviality will affect her. But even if these problems are real, so too is the problem of having death, and a very obviously premature death, just around the corner. There's a lot that the good life promises that is, for Rosie, fast falling out of reach. And given these are the options it may be less clear that, even granted immortality's downside, taking the elixir would, for her, be a mistake.

Will she, though, like EM, in the end, be bored to death? Remember, it's been agreed that suicide, an exit strategy, isn't an option. If in time she'll want nothing more, nothing other than to die, and if death is forever unavailable, then opting for the elixir will turn out to have been a profound mistake. But this overlooks something. For even if there will come a time when she'd regret immortality, and wish she were dead, that time might not last forever. Her mood could change. And EM, had she taken her second dose, might have found that some of the pleasures in life later returned.

So it may be that even if an immortal life is peculiarly different to the life we live today, even if, too, it ought to seem to us a vastly inferior life, it might nevertheless be better than nothing at all. It's unlikely, of course, that you'll be offered an elixir just at the time you're about to die. Like Sammy, you might be faced with a difficult decision when things are in full swing. But go back to the religious perspective, and suppose there is a heaven. Martyrs apart, you'll go there, if at all, and start your new life, at what would in any case be the end of this one. It may be, then, that heaven is better than nothing, and something you could, with reason, hope for.

Further Finessing

Assume, though, that Williams is right. An immortal life, because of the difficulties listed above, is not something we could reasonably want for ourselves. Paint it in its most glowing colours, and death would still be better.

Perhaps, though, we could make still further adjustments to what immortality might be like, in order to avoid this conclusion. One way is to consider the links, insisted on by Williams, and emphasized again above, between boredom and frivolity on the one hand, and the persistence of character, on the other. It's because we want to be more or less the same person that boredom and a lack of seriousness set in. So what if we give up on this wish to stay the same?

Ideas about reincarnation might be of some help here. You live forever, but in a series of different forms. And just as the mouse knows nothing of the donkey, neither do you know of the woodcutter you were, and nor will the star traveller you'll in time become know anything of you today. The problem with reincarnation is that it's very hard to see how two people, centuries and continents apart, with neither minds nor bodies in common, can really be one and the same. But perhaps we can get over that:

The Rejuvenation Chamber. Making babies the old way, giving birth, growing them up, all this is time-consuming, messy, and expensive. And it's no longer necessary. Who needs new people, when the old ones just run and run? And since they perfected the Mark II chamber this is exactly what happens. People first live their 80 or so years in the normal way – family, job, hobbies, the works. Then they're given an anaesthetic, put into the chamber, and within an hour or two are rejuvenated. What does this mean? It means that their bodies seem to lose about 60 years, while their minds, though they can speak, are rational, and quick to learn, are otherwise unformed. And then, 60 years later, they do it again.

Is this immortality? There is little doubt that the inventors of the chamber have done away with death. The very same body, with the very same brain just goes on and on. There is little doubt, too, that these rejuvenated lives are, in several important respects, normal human lives. The problems that affected EM don't get a hold here. But does the chamber really extend the one life, or does it instead create a series of new lives, though all of them with parts in common? That might be a hard question, but even without answering it, there are useful things that can be said. What the machine does, as well as renewing the body, is obliterate all that is distinctive about the mind. You come out knowing nothing of what you were like when you went in. Your knowledge of the world, your tastes, you character all need to be reformed. This is why, when you see Chelsea draw with Juventus yet again, you're not bored. And it's why, when you're choosing between politics and rock music, your decision is of momentous importance.

Yet these problems with immortality are solved only at considerable cost. Even if it is the same person who both enters and exits the chamber, these disruptions to character and memory are so predictable, and so severe, that it's unclear how anyone could think the procedure has anything at all to commend it. You don't die, but, as in an irreversible coma, what happens is as bad as death. And it's no wonder that Williams, in considering this sort of serial life, finds no improvement on our lives as we live them now.

But there might be further finessing. Suppose we live not, as here, one life rudely abutting the next, but what are in effect a string of overlapping lives. Won't this solve the problem, and give us, at last, something worth having? But, then, just what are these overlapping lives? How does it work?

The Seamless Life. Ernie Morecambe, like Emilia Marty, was born 337 years ago. Like her he has, magically, shown little sign of ageing. Those meeting him for the first time think he's in his late thirties. But unlike her, Ernie isn't the least bit bored with life. Tell him even an old joke, and he's likely to laugh. Show him a dance routine, and rather than mutter that he's been through it far too many times already, he's willing to give it a go. He may be an old dog, but it seems there's a constant supply of new tricks. How come? It's his memory. Ernie has only hazy memories of things that happened more than 30 years ago. Another five years, and it's forgotten completely. And this is always true. He's always leaving the past behind.

It's as if Ernie lives in something like a bubble of time. Unlike you and me, he'll never have reason to believe that annihilation is just around the corner. Whatever his plans for the next five, the next ten or twenty years, he'll still be there to realize them. But, unlike Elina Makropulos, deep and persistent forgetfulness means that Ernie is unable to look back upon, and so unable to be prisoner to, a near endless past.

Boredom isn't a problem then. Give him the works of Shakespeare, and he just can't remember having read them a dozen or more times already. No more than schoolchildren does he know already what will happen to Macbeth, or whether Cordelia will live or die. Nor is his life any the more frivolous, his choices any the less weighty, than ours. Though he knows that in one sense he'll live forever, for certainly he'll never die, Ernie knows too that he'll never have to hold together, like an ordinary immortal, a complete mix of experiences. For suppose he thinks there's no urgency to a Russian tour – he can do it, and maybe with an improved act, in a hundred years time. But he hasn't really this long, if he wants some activity or experience to mesh with the life he's living now. Nor, we can suppose, is there anything complex or unsettling about Ernie's relation to character. He reads diaries of his former selves, just as we might read diaries of our ancestors or foot soldiers from some old war, and finds often that there are similarities between those people then and himself now. But he doesn't remember anything of what happened then, and thinks of himself as a different person. And so, unlike EM, by the time he's done all that it makes sense for someone of 37 to do, he's already moving on.

All in all, then, Ernie's life avoids the pitfalls of immortality. But this is in large part because, in an important sense, he isn't immortal. What is unappealing about living on, what makes it in some ways a curse, is something that the defects of memory allows Ernie to avoid. On the other hand, he avoids as well the badness of death. It will never seem to

Ernie that there's no time left. Take both sides into account, then, and this seamless life might be something to hope for.

A Get-out Clause

Let's go back to an earlier point. If there is an afterlife of the religious kind, an existence in heaven or hell, the chances are it will go on forever. But can it really be the same with an elixir? Can we really imagine a life on earth from which there is absolutely no way out? It's hard to believe in this. Even Achilles had his heel. When I read about Superman, I find it difficult to work out whether he's genuinely immortal or not. And Elina Makropulos was getting, at best, 300 year bursts of eternal life. Realistically, a human being will always, somehow or other, be able to die. So now imagine this. You're offered the elixir. But you know that while it gives you protection from ordinary deaths, there is always a get out, an exit strategy, to hand. Imagine this and, surely, the objections to taking it fall away.

Perhaps. Certainly it's better this way. But suicide, when what is ended is an immortal life, would be such a momentous decision, that for most of us it would be extremely hard to make it. Why so? Ending life always has the same result – finish things, and you are forever, ceaselessly, irreversibly dead. But for most of us, deciding on suicide is deciding only to live a few years, maybe just weeks or days, less. For most of us the writing is already on the wall, and it merely hastens an already inevitably end. But for the immortal, to opt to die is to leave behind an infinity of years. That's a much bigger decision. And we can guess that it might not come easy.

Should I Take the Elixir of Life?

There is no elixir. Maybe there never will be. Maybe too there's no heaven. But as well as wondering, as many of us do, what will happens after death, it's certainly worth wondering too, what we should hope will happen. And even if annihilation seems bad, the oft-mooted alternative, an immortal life, isn't obviously any better. For make the details of such a life as attractive as possible and there's still the danger that in the long run, boredom, apathy, a sense of alienation from people and from things, is bound to set in.

So at least it is for EM and Williams. And like them, I think I'd prefer eventually to die, rather than to live forever. But I'm not sure that this isn't just a point about me. I'm not sure, that is, that someone who opts for immortality is necessarily making a big mistake. They need to recognise that the endless life will be unaccountably different from the life they lead today, and recognise too that they'll need to become a very different sort of person in order to cope with it. But people can change, and change a lot, and so long as there's enough persistence of character and memory then the mortal, and immortal, may well be one and the same.

Some people will be troubled by this, thinking that there's got to be a clearer and more definitive answer. Either immortality will be bad for us, however good it is or, at its best, it's something we'd be fools to give up on. Perhaps these people are right. But at the moment I can't see that they are.

Chapter Seven

Who's Who?

OK, then, if I'm not me, who the hell am I?
(Arnold Schwarzenegger, as Doug Quaid in *Total Recall*)

We all change. Both physically and psychologically we're very different at ages 5, 35 and 70. But for most of us, and for most of the time, there's no doubt that we remain the same person throughout. Our identity, who we are, is in many ways resilient. And yet it seems that there must be some limits here, and that certain changes would threaten this identity, turning us into someone else, a different person, or, as in the final stages of Alzheimer's disease, someone who's no longer really a person at all. The question, then, is how far, and in what ways might I change, and yet continue to be me? Or, to put this another way, what is involved in a particular person's persisting through time?

This is a good question on various counts. Religion often envisages big changes at or around the time of death. But perhaps those changes are too great, in fact, for a particular person to survive. So even if there is someone, after death, who resembles me in certain respects, that person might still not be me. And science, technology, medicine together aim at big changes for many of us. But again they might be too big. Imagine brain or mind transplants, or the freezing and thawing of cryogenics, or the speed-of-light travel in *Star Trek* or in the film *The Fly*. Even if, after all this, there's certainly someone who exists, it might not be the person we think it is, the person we started out with, and were trying to save or to move. Unless we can decide who's who, when a particular person survives, and when they are replaced by someone else, then a lot of what we might pray for, or pay for, could be a waste of time.

The Mind View

Put the question differently again. You come across someone, just call him A, on Tuesday. And then you meet someone, B, on Thursday.

What would have to be true for A and B to be the same person? What connections or similarities between them would there need to be? This isn't the question of how you might tell that two people are one the same – it isn't a question about how we can know things. Rather it's a more basic question, about what it is for the two to be one, or what is involved in identity over time.

And here's a popular answer: if the mind is the same, the person is the same. So if A and B have the same mind, then they're one and the same person, whatever the physical links and physical similarities between them. Consider this imaginary case:

The Hard Drive. It's Wednesday, and Salman and Hanif are involved in a car crash. Hanif hits the wheel and suffers instant and fatal brain damage. But his body is otherwise undamaged. Salman's injuries are far more extensive, but when the doctors reach him he's still alive. They need to act quickly. They hook Hanif's body to a respirator, and get to work on Salman, recording, while there's still time, the contents of his brain onto the computer's hard drive. Meanwhile, they repair Hanif's brain, its contents all lost, with bits of jelly and plastic. Then they transfer the contents of Salman's brain from the hard drive to this repaired brain. All this has gone remarkably smoothly, and by Thursday morning they're able to switch off the respirator and offer this person – he looks like Hanif and thinks like Salman – some breakfast.

Who gets the breakfast? On the mind view it's definitely Salman. Why? Because this person thinks like Salman, and remembers what Salman did. And it doesn't matter that no part of Salman's body has survived, that it's already been cremated, and the ashes floated down the Thames. The fact that his mind survives, and continues to operate more or less as before, is enough to ensure that Salman himself continues to exist.

Is the mind view right? A lot of people will think so. For a lot of people think that what matters about us, what makes us the person we are, just is that we have certain memories, certain beliefs, a tendency to act and think in certain ways. And this is why there seems to be some comfort, and nothing too puzzling, in the idea of life after death as a disembodied soul; and why, as well, reincarnation as a deer or a seagull can seem attractive so long as we assume our human mind somehow fuses with the animal body. The mind view sits well, also, with our reactions to stories in books, on TV or in films. Gregor Samsa in Kafka's *Metamorphosis* wakes up to discover he's stuck inside a giant beetle. And we agree this is what's happened – it's a tale about an unfortunate person, rather than a deluded insect. The Doctor, in *Doctor Who*, finds himself in a new body, though with the same clothes, every few years. He thinks, and we think, it's the same person going on and on just because his mind, and his memories are, more or less the same.

Admittedly, these stories aren't altogether like the story of Salman and Hanif. For it might be that Samsa's human body doesn't just disappear, but is transformed into a beetle body. And it might be, similarly, that the Doctor's body is somehow regenerated, rather than being replaced by a completely new and different body. There might, as in many of Ovid's tales, be continuity, although a surprising degree of change, in physical stuff. But I don't think this detail is crucial to our understanding – we'd get it either way. And it seems fairly clear that the Teletransporter in *Star Trek* does cause one body to disappear completely, and a new body to be formed in a different place. But we don't think a new person is created – because this person has the same mind as Kirk or Spock, we think that it's Kirk or Spock who survives.

Of course, we recognize, most of us, that these are just stories. And we mostly accept that any beliefs we might have in an afterlife fall some way short of proven fact. So it may turn out to be impossible to separate minds from bodies, and then to house them elsewhere, or let them just float free. Even so, it may be that these stories tell us something about ourselves, about what is important to us, and about the kinds of things we think that, in essence, we are.

Another aspect of the mind view certainly isn't fiction, however. Perhaps we'll never have minds without bodies, but too often we have bodies without minds. People die. Before they die they sometimes lose their mind completely, as when, after an accident, they fall into a coma or persistent vegetative state, or almost completely, as with the later stages of Alzheimer's or some other degenerative disease. Think just about the cases where life goes on. There is a living human being here, but is there a person? Would you still exist?

The mind view says no. There's someone alive on Tuesday, and someone alive on Thursday. If the mind's the same, then the person's the same. But if there's no mind, then whether or not there's a human being, dead or alive, there's no person at all. And if there's a different mind, there's a different person. So consider:

You Are What You Eat. There was a famous case in San Francisco in the late 1970s. Though he admitted killing the mayor and the supervisor, Dan White denied murder. And it seemed to some that he was blaming junk food, and Twinkie bars in particular, for that fateful loss of control. Too much sugar. But that's old hat. The new bars, Slinkies, are way stronger. Two or three of these and there's a complete personality shift – you remember nothing of your past, and you behave altogether differently, throwing your weight about, swearing, wearing bad clothes.

Slinkies affect you badly. But how badly? Do they alter your behaviour? Or do they cause you, perhaps temporarily, no longer to exist? The mind view holds that each of us is constituted by our psychology, and that, in turn, comprises our thoughts, beliefs, character, dispositions and memory. When they are all gone, we too are gone, whether or not the body continues. Eat enough candy, and you might simply disappear. Now that will seem a strange view, but it does gain some support from our reactions to many cases involving a radical personality shift. Suppose a friend of yours is captured by an evil hypnotist, or someone with a stock of psychotropic drugs, and then persuaded that she's the reincarnation of Attila the Hun. Under the sway of this belief she performs a variety of unspeakable acts. The next day the drug wears off, or someone snaps their fingers, and your friend returns to her normal state, unaware of all she's done. Certainly the law wouldn't hold her responsible, but would busy itself with searching for the hypnotists or druggists instead. And most of us would agree that it wasn't her fault. This doesn't prove, of course, that either the law or common sense actually believes that someone might temporarily cease to exist. But it does give that idea some support, and suggests, I think, that the mind view isn't obviously flawed.

It might be stronger in other cases. Imagine a séance. It's a country house party and, tired of playing bridge, they want to find out if there's anybody there. There's port, cigars, the curtains drawn, the lights down. Mrs O'Cady soon goes into a trance and begins to speak, convincingly, as if she's the owner's great-uncle, Cecil, the one killed in the Boer War. Such things usually last for five or ten minutes. But this time it's impossible to bring her round, and thereafter, until the day she dies, she remembers nothing of her own life, but continues always to talk and behave as if she had first-hand knowledge of Mafeking. In this situation, where the personality shift is permanent, and where we can identify this new personality with a particular individual, we'd be even more inclined, I think, to say that the first person has disappeared (either completely, or at least we know not where) and has been replaced by the second. So it's the mind, rather than the body, that determines a person's identity.

The Body View

Some people think this is all wrong. Someone on Tuesday, someone on Thursday. If and only if it's the same physical thing, the same animal, the same human being, on both days is the person the same. It's the body, rather than the mind, that does the work in establishing personal identity.

It's worth sorting out a bit more of the detail here. Supporters of the body view allow, of course, that bodies can change. Murgatroyd, on Tuesday, feels unwell. She has, successfully, a heart transplant on Wednesday. She still exists on Thursday even though her body isn't the same throughout. So how much can the body change while the person remains the same? A lot of people think the brain is the crucial component, and that we can in principle replace parts other than the brain without compromising a person's existence. Another question concerns life. Suppose the operation is a failure. Does she still exist on Thursday? Most people will say no, and insist that when we die the person ceases to exist. I survive so long as this body continues to live and breathe. But that's really all that matters. I survive whatever I'm thinking about, however much I've forgotten, no matter what I seem to remember.

We care a lot about what people think and believe, how they behave, how much of their lives they remember. Supporters of the body view accept this. So they accept that it's very hard if someone important to us suffers some sort of mental calamity. But as you continue to exist, although in a worse state, if you lose your legs in an accident so, similarly, if you lose your mind. And of course what the body view says here is supported by everyday reactions. Three relatives are involved in a boating accident. One drowns, the second has such a degree of brain damage that they are thereafter in a persistent vegetative state, the third makes a partial recovery, but has no more mental capacity than a one-year-old child. For most of us, three tragedies, but only in the first will it be relatively easy to say the person no longer exists, to feel that we can draw a line, to move on. And think about films like *The Invasion of the Body Snatchers*, or *The Stepford Wives*, or various Dracula movies. Ordinary people are taken over, their bodies intact, their minds zombified, by aliens, vampires, or all-American husbands. There's no going back, no chance of restoring these people to their earlier condition. And even more people are threatened. But though it would be for the best, it's hard to write these people off, to accept they no longer exist, and to kill the things they've now become. It's hard not to think that so long as the living body survives, then the person survives.

Yet is it only others who continue to exist though their minds are gone? Or do we think in the same way about ourselves? Bernard Williams asks us to consider the sort of situation that occurs in the following example:

> *Beyond Torture*. Bad things might happen. Dr Sachs, the sadist, captures all three of them. He tells Julian that he's going to be tortured. Wires will be attached to various parts of his body and the current turned on. George learns that first she'll be made to forget everything that's ever happened to her, next drained of all aspects of her character and then infected with a set of fake memories and a fake character instead. Messing with the body and messing with the mind are both bad, and Julian and George are both afraid. And Timmy? He learns that he's first going to partner George, getting a fake mind in place of the real one. And then he'll be set beside Julian, wires will be attached, and he'll be tortured. He too is afraid.

Sachs is good at what he does, and he certainly gives all three something to worry about. But just how scared should Timmy be? Is his fate just as bad as George's, or is it even worse? On the mind view, Sachs is going to destroy George and replace her with someone else. Maybe he'll reverse this later, having kept her details on his laptop, maybe not. But if this is right, and if the same thing happens to Timmy, then any subsequent torture is a problem not for him, but for the new person.

Williams thinks that most of us would be afraid, and would be right to be afraid, were we to be threatened with treatment like Timmy's. But not simply because we'll get what George gets. It's bad to be tortured. And it remains bad if, beforehand, your memories are destroyed, fake ones are inserted, and your character is changed. We exist so long as our living body exists, and what happens to that body happens to us.

Taking Sides

Which view is right? Am I my mind, or my body? Do I exist so long as, and only so long as thoughts, memories, dispositions like these continue, or do I exist so long as, and only so long as, this body remains alive? It's surely an important question as to who or what we are, and one that deserves an answer.

And it's a hard question. Before introducing the torture case that I've outlined above, Williams discusses another case, something like this:

Pain or Gain. It's one of those weird TV game shows. Hanna and Sylvie are both told that one of them will be given some money, the other 10 minutes of torture. They're not friends, and each wants money for herself, torture for the other. But this comes later. First, they have to enter, and then leave, a mind swap machine. One of those leaving will have Hanna's body and, apparently, Sylvie's mind, while the other will have Sylvie's body and, or so it seems, Hanna's mind. Before they go in the machine Sylvie is asked which one should be tortured, which rewarded. She thinks about it. 'I hate torture. Give me – my mind, Hanna's body – the money. Torture her – Hanna's mind, my body. That way, I won't feel a thing.'

It may be a bit hard on Hanna, but most of us will think Sylvie's made the right decision here. She is where her mind is. And this case is quite like that involving Hanif and Salman, except here there are two survivors, rather than one. Yet if Salman survives, but in Hanif's body, surely Sylvie survives so long as, and where her mind survives. The problem, though, is that it's like Timmy's case as well, except again that there are two people rather than one. Timmy's mind is messed with, and then he's tortured. But doesn't the same thing happen to Sylvie? If, as it seems, Timmy's right to be frightened by what's going to happen to his living conscious body, then surely Sylvie's wrong to think that so long as her mind is reshaped, torture for her body isn't torture for her. But now if she is wrong to think this, then Salman's friends are wrong to think that Salman has survived the crash. He might believe he's Salman, but it's really Hanif, though much changed.

Put the different cases together in this way, and the difficulty in deciding between the mind view and body view becomes more pronounced. We want to say, surely Timmy is right to fear the torture. But we want to say as well, surely Salman survives. But it seems we can't say both. And as for Sylvie, happy for others to be tortured . . .

What is needed, in order to get out of this mess, are some more questions. Answer these, and maybe we can be clearer about personal identity.

Do Numbers Count?

In most ordinary cases, people just go on from day to day with no threats to, or puzzles about, their identity. Often, when things go wrong, there's only the one person involved. Andrew had a bad trip, some dodgy dealer on the South Side, and though he's still alive, people wonder whether he's really with us. No one asks if he's someone else. Sometimes there's two, and we wonder if, after the séance, we're talking to O'Cady, or to Cecil. There is, apparently, the body of the one, and the mind of the other. It's the same with the aftermath of the crash, where it seems that Salman might survive in Hanif's body.

It's worth thinking about whether and how the number of people involved makes a difference to these identity problems. Some defenders of the body view appeal to worries about numbers in support of their position. They think a problem with minds is that they could crop up all over the place:

> *The Harder Drive.* There were three people in the car. Like Hanif, Nasreen's body remains, but his brain too has to be repaired with jelly and plastic. Salman's body is ruined, but with the contents of his brain stored on the computer, doctors are able to patch up Hanif's body and brain, and programme this living organism with Salman's mind. But they worry that this operation might be a failure. And so, to be on the safe side, and as the information is still on the computer, they programme Nasreen's body in the same way. But both operations are successful, so there's a double order of breakfast. In one bed, someone who looks like Hanif and who thinks he is Salman, eating boiled eggs, and drinking tea. In another, someone looking like Nasreen, thinking like Salman, with coffee and croissants.

On the mind view, there are now two Salmans. There's just one person, who happens now to exist in two different places. But surely, the body view people say, this can't be right. Start with the breakfast. Why are they eating different things? Why hasn't Salman simply ordered his usual twice over, whatever it is? Well, what we want to eat is in part determined by what our body tells us, and different bodies will presumably tell us different things. Maybe Salman used to eat cereal every day, so he's somewhat surprised by both choices. But this is just a start. From here on the two Salmans are going to become more and more different, with what they think, how they act, what they plan next, and what they later remember, all shaped by their increasingly different experiences. Give it a few months, and anyone meeting them would have no doubt they were two different people, even though they each seem to think that, until recently, the very same things had happened to them both. As there are two different people here, and as neither has a stronger claim to be Salman than the other, so then neither, it seems, can be Salman.

He didn't survive the crash, even if, for a while at least, both Hanif and Nasreen appear to act and think like him.

Supporters of the body view are certainly on to something here. There is a problem in thinking you survive so long as your mind survives. A double survival isn't a bonus, but a challenge to the belief that you persist through time. But then these supporters press their attack still further. If we finish up with the situation described in *Harder Drive*, then Salman doesn't survive. But then he doesn't survive, either, in the earlier situation, where there are only two crash victims. Salman's survival in Hanif's body can't depend on the presence and fortune of a third person, Nasreen. More generally, whether someone on Thursday is the same person as someone on Wednesday must depend on the links between them alone. It can't depend on what does or doesn't happen to someone else. And so even the possibility of a double survival counts against the mind view.

One worry I have about this is that it may work against the body view as well. Suppose first that what matters is, as suggested earlier, just a part of the body, the brain. So you survive if your brain is transplanted into a different body. But the brain isn't a soul, isn't a simple indivisible thing, and as a matter of clinical fact you'd survive equally well if less than the whole brain were transplanted. So now imagine:

> *Knock Outs*. Ken and Joe have slugged it through to the last round. It's hard to say who's ahead on points. And then, with only seconds to go, it's a double knock out, they both collapse, and neither regains consciousness. There's uproar in the crowd, and in the rush to get the story out Henry, sports reporter for WFXM, is crushed. All three end up in the same hospital, the boxers both with fatal brain damage, Henry still with a glimmer of hope. But it's only a glimmer, with his body ruined, and some injuries to his head. Doctors believe, though, that the left side of his brain is still intact, and, as one half alone is enough to operate a body, and to sustain a mind, they transfer this into Ken's body. By a whisker, then, Henry survives. But then a junior doctor looks again at the right side of Henry's brain, and sees that the injuries there are much less than they first seemed. Working against the clock, he transfers this to Joe's body. Guaranteeing that Henry survives twice over, the doctor is confident his promotion is now in the bag.

Yet he shouldn't rush to celebrate. As before, two cannot be one, and what seems a double success is in fact a single failure. Henry is no more. Suppose the doctor trips on a loose tile, and drops this second half of Henry's brain. But if the objection worked against the mind view, it works as well here. Whether or not Henry survives in Ken's body can't depend on what happens elsewhere. It can't depend on whether or not a spare part of his brain is successfully transplanted.

Suppose you think more than half a brain is needed. You might even think we need the whole body. A science-fiction film. Sasha works hard, returns home, goes to bed, falls asleep. In the night his body mysteriously divides, and two people wake the next morning. Two cannot be one, and so Sasha hasn't survived. You might think, though, that if identity is lost when such division is occurred, it is precarious, at best, throughout. Whether or not the person who wakes in the morning is the same as the one who falls asleep in the evening ought not to depend on the happy accident of divisions not occurring.

In the cases described here we end with two people, each of whom can claim, on very similar grounds, to be the original person. In other cases the grounds might be different. Even so, it will be hard to choose between them. But forget people for a while, and think instead about:

Ships. The Ruritanians want to have a navy. They buy a ship from the Cubans, rename it *Adelaide* and are very proud. But so they're ready for war, they dismantle the ship completely, clean and repair all the parts, checking for wear, and then rebuild it. At the same time they draw up a renovation programme, agreeing in the future to replace parts, one by one, before they wear out completely. And over the next five years the parts are gradually replaced with exact replicas, supplied by the Cubans, until at the end of that time none of the original parts remain. What happens to these parts? Just for emergencies, the parts are carefully numbered, and stored in a warehouse.

Can we dismantle and rebuild a ship? Surely we can. And the rebuilt ship is the *Adelaide* and not some copy. Can we replace parts of a ship? Of course. And there seems to be no reason to suppose we can't, on a rolling programme of repair, replace all the parts. No part in particular is crucial to a ship's identity, and there's no good reason to think we can replace only 49 per cent, or 99 per cent, or indeed any other proportion of parts before identity is lost. So far so good, but the problem is in the warehouse. Because of a further threat of war the Ruritanians decide they need to double their navy. So they take the parts from the warehouse and assemble them into a ship. Which ship? Surely this is the dismantled and reassembled *Adelaide*. But surely too, and just as surely, the other ship is the *Adelaide*, the one that's been in existence throughout, now with all its original parts replaced. One has become two.

The situation with the ship is somewhat similar to that involving Timmy, Hanna and, before Nasreen came along, Salman. We think someone might, like Timmy, have their mind messed with, and still survive. We think as well that someone might get a completely new body, like Salman, and still survive. But then if we're happy with all this, there's a problem for Hanna, who appears now to survive twice over — there's her body, with a messed-up mind, and there's her mind, in what is for her a completely new body. She's become two.

It seems, then, that numbers do count. The more people, and parts of people, the more ships and bits of ships are involved, the more puzzling, often, things become. We believe the person with Hanif's body is Salman. But then we find out about someone else, Nasreen, discover what happens to him, and we no longer believe this. And that's a puzzle. But, as I've suggested, it's not a puzzle that counts just against the mind view. It affects the body view as well.

Is It All or Nothing?

Someone on Tuesday, someone on Thursday. Is it the same person or someone else? Suppose on Tuesday you need a dangerous operation. Sometimes people having these operations suffer a degree of brain damage. It might happen to you. And you wonder if you'll survive the operation, and still be around on Thursday. It's very tempting to think that there must be answers to questions like these. Either it will be the same person, or someone else. Either you'll survive, or you won't. There's no room for half-measures, and identity is all or nothing.

But perhaps it's wrong to think this. Perhaps there are cases where it's not only that we don't know, but that there just is no clear-cut answer to who a person is, or whether a person survives. Think about another ship:

Men o' War. The Cubans capture a ship from the French. It's a frigate, light, built of the best French oak, and highly manoeuvrable under sail. There's some damage from cannonballs on the quarterdeck, and they set about repairing it. And then over the years the repairs continue. But the Cubans aren't wedded to the past, and don't insist on exact replica parts. If improvements can be made, they make them. And so gradually they add metal parts, first as cladding, later as replacement for the main timbers. There's an auxiliary engine, then a bigger one, and later still the masts and sails are removed. The entire ship becomes longer and broader as well, and what began as frigate is now reclassified as a battleship. And then, short of money, they sell it to the Ruritanians.

How many ships are involved? Surely the ship they first capture is different from that they later sell. A wooden frigate is one thing, an iron battleship another. And this is so even if the former is transformed into the latter. Or think of a potter who with the same lump of clay first makes a tall vase but then, dissatisfied, turns it into a low bowl. The vase is one thing, the bowl another. Even so, there isn't a moment when the first ship is transformed into the second, or when the vase becomes the bowl. It's a gradual process. Someone asks, 'Is this a frigate?' Early on the answer is yes, later on it's no. But there's a period in the middle when this question doesn't have a yes/no answer.

It's the same as well, when things go out of existence. Imagine a modern artist whose 'work', in a fashionable gallery, is to eat a dining table. Wood isn't particularly digestible, so this takes well over a year. On day one the table is intact. He takes his first bite on day two and his last five hundred days later. There's certainly a table in the gallery for the first ten days, certainly no table for the last ten. But there's a period in the middle when the question, 'Is this a table?' can't get a yes/no answer.

And surely it's the same with people. The mad scientist captures Tom Cruise and gradually turns him into an exact copy of Nicole Kidman. Every day he makes some alteration to his body, a little bit taller, a little bit curvier, and every day some alteration to his mind, deleting some memories and adding others, or replacing male dominance with feminine guile. At the end of the process Tom no longer exists, but we'd be hard pushed to say exactly when this happens. 'Is it the same person?' like, 'Is it the same ship?' might have no yes/no answer. Another scientist, less imaginative, is concerned simply to make Harrison Ford disappear. He captures him, and gradually removes bits of his body, and bits of his mind, keeping the remains alive on respirators and in Petri dishes, until there's nothing left.

There are two objections to these analogies. First, except in a meta-phorical sense, ships and tables have no souls. Perhaps people do. If we have souls, then it may be that I exist so long as, and just where, my soul exists. And if the soul is a simple and indivisible thing, then, assuming as well that they cannot be duplicated, there are no complications: it either exists or it doesn't, and the question of whether I exist always gets a yes/no answer. But, to repeat a point from an earlier chapter, there isn't good reason to think that people have, or are, souls. The second objection fastens on one version of the body view, and tries to make something of it. Everyone agrees that some bits of the body can be removed, and maybe replaced, without affecting who I am. But a lot of people think the brain is special. Keep it, and I remain. Replace it, and I'm gone. So if the scientist preserves Tom's brain throughout, then Tom continues to exist, no matter what he thinks, or what he looks like. Let's suppose, then, that as well as interfering with the rest of his body, he gradually replaces his brain, bit by bit. That, after all, might be the easiest way of interfering with his mind. So if Tom is to be identified with his brain, then, at the end of the day, he no longer exists. Yet as his brain is replaced only gradually, his ceasing to exist is, likewise, a gradual process. And so there'll be a lengthy period within this devilish procedure when the question, 'Is this or is it not Tom?', just has no answer. Similarly with Harrison. Gradually, his brain disappears.

These are fictional cases, certainly. But with Alzheimer's, in too many real cases, the mind does gradually disappear. And though we're still a long way from anything like the situations in *Robocop*, spare-part surgery is now increasingly common. So the difference between fictional and real cases is one of degree, rather than kind. Perhaps we should admit that, even now, identity isn't all or nothing.

A Solution? And a Problem?

Should we put weight on the mind, or the body? Does duplication, and the threat of duplication, threaten our survival? Is our continued existence sometimes, or always, a matter of degree? Some philosophers have suggested a way to deal with such questions. We should adopt a *closest continuer* account of identity. It goes like this. Which of the people around on Thursday is the same as the person we were concerned with on Tuesday? Usually there's no problem here, but sometimes there is. If there are two people, both of whom can make something of a case, choose the one with the strongest case. If the strongest case is still very weak, then Tuesday's person no longer exists. If two cases are equally strong then, again, the person no longer exists.

So think about Kirk, in the Teletransporter. If all goes well, he disappears on Earth, and reappears on Mars. But they forget the 10 billion mile service, and there are problems on the next trip. He reappears on both planets. That might be the end of his existence, but it may be that there are reasons to prefer one Kirk to the other. Suppose one of them is ghostly, or deranged, or the next day turns into an intergalactic monster. Then the other one is Kirk.

And think about some of the cases described above. If we don't reassemble the stored parts, the renovated ship is the *Adelaide*. If we never start on a replacement programme, but simply take apart, clean up and reconstruct the one ship, that is the *Adelaide*. We only get a problem when the procedures are combined. Similarly, Hanif survives the crash, Timmy withstands the perversities of Dr Sachs, while Hanna, splitting into two, goes out of existence. And Hanif goes out of existence, too, if Nasreen is in the car, and two bodies are reprogrammed.

Perhaps this isn't quite right. Perhaps a continuously existing ship takes priority over one that is disassembled and reassembled. Perhaps the body trumps the mind, so that Hanif might have gone to heaven, but it's Salman who eats breakfast. Yet these are details. And the closest continuer account has shown us the way forward. It's shown us how to approach these puzzles about identity, and how its problems can be solved.

I think there's a lot in this. But there's an important qualification that needs to be made. It's a qualification that bears upon much of the business of philosophy, and on many of the questions asked in this book.

It's almost always tempting, when asked a question, to take it at face value, and to think it has some answer. There are, perhaps some obvious non-questions – 'What colour is the number 7?' – and some well-known tricks – 'When did you stop beating your wife?' – but for the most part questions look to be, and are taken as, straightforward. This, though, is a temptation best resisted. If asked how the universe began, we might think on the one hand about the big bang, and on the other about God. But perhaps we should consider instead that it might have had no beginning, and so demand a prior question airing that as a possibility. Similarly, the sort of question popular now on TV shows, 'Which are the ten greatest books of all time?', should probably be shelved in favour of asking whether the very idea of greatest books makes sense. But now many philosophical questions, and the reactions of many when asked those questions, are similarly steeped in assumptions, many of which shouldn't be allowed an easy passage. Socrates was always searching for the real nature of justice, piety, courage and so on, and that approach continues with hardly a break, so that a lot of contemporary discussion is focused on giving, for example, a definition of knowledge, or art, or truth. I'm not suggesting that this sort of thing is wrong in principle, and it can after all be a lot of fun to come up with a definition, find some problem case, real or imaginary, tweak the definition to fit, discover a further problem, and so on through the greater part of one's career. But there's certainly reason now and again to stop and ask about the legitimacy of these assumptions that things have natures, that there are definitions to be found, that we can say precisely what such and such is. There is reason, then, rather than attempt a straightforward solution to an alleged problem, to ask first whether the problem is real, and whether a solution is needed. And that too is a part of what philosophy is about.

Go back to the questions about identity. I've suggested that sometimes we can, while other times we can't say who on Thursday is the same person as someone on Tuesday. Many times the answer is altogether obvious, sometimes the closest continuer account will adjudicate between two candidates, while at other times there may just be no answer to whether or not Tuesday's person survives. But now it's important, I think, to realize that there's no crucial difference here. You might think that in those cases where there is a clear answer – it's certain that I'm the same person I was yesterday, and it's certain, too, that none of those Elvis impersonators is really Elvis – this is because there is something, some deep, though here accessible, fact about identity, that makes this answer correct and clear. And so, in the cases where there is no answer, that deep fact is missing. But this isn't right. When, with good reason, we're confident that someone survives a night's sleep, or a minor operation, or a knock on the head, this isn't because we've grasped some profound metaphysical fact about identity that remains, throughout this period, the same. Rather it's because the ordinary surface facts about what is happening here – the degree, the normality, the causes of any changes that might occur – provide these reasons, and make appropriate this confidence. But in other cases – and thankfully there are fewer of them – the ordinary surface facts are different, they destroy reasons for confidence, and leave things up in the air.

And so the closest continuer account, even if I seem to favour it, doesn't give us the real truth about identity, and doesn't amount to a theorized position that we need to accept and follow. Rather, it's simply that it approximates reasonably closely to the kinds of things that, already, we think and say and do.

Who's Who?

Mostly there's no problem here, and it's easy to tell whether the person we see at the end of the week is the same person we saw at the beginning.

But in other cases, both real and imaginary, there is a problem. People change, strange things happen, and there are times when change, or circumstances, can cause us to question the identity of the person before us. How to settle things? Even if it takes a while to sort out the details, both the mind view and the body view offer, in the end, fairly clear-cut criteria here. Apply them, and the question of whether it's the same person, or someone else, finds its answer.

The problem now, though, is that neither view manages altogether to convince. Though they each have their good points, there are serious difficulties facing both. Each of them has to fend off the challenge from the other, they're both subject to pressure from various puzzle cases, perhaps especially those involving duplication, and the body view can be involved in arbitrary distinctions about just how much body, or brain, is needed to keep identity intact. But how serious are these problems? Might we, in spite of them, prove that one of these views is right? Could one of them be right even though we can't prove it? Elsewhere, of course, there's no difficulty with the idea that the truth should be well hidden — we know very little about climate change, the workings of the brain, or how the universe began. But surely it's not at all clear how questions of identity over time — either for relatively simple things ships or vases, or for the greater complexity of people like you and me — could, similarly be deeply mysterious and perplexing. It's not clear, then, how, given their various difficulties, either the mind view or the body view could be correct. And although it's possible to bite the bullet, and stick with one or other of these criteria come what may, it seems there are reasons to look elsewhere.

The closest continuer view, I've suggested, fares better. Take it on a case-by-case basis, and its verdicts reveal a better fit with our everyday intuitions about identity, and where it's to be found. It, too, has problems, but they come at one remove, in meeting the objections of those — and they're many — who think the situation vis-à-vis identity must be clearer, sharper, than this view allows. And, in particular, the objection is that there surely must in every case be a definite answer to whether or not a given person survives. Without this, there's still some way to go.

Yet consider again two problem cases, one imaginary, the other real. Some believe that Salman survives as his mind survives, while others think that the continuity of his body and his repaired brain mean that the person eating breakfast is Hanif. But they'll all agree that we've Hanif's body and, in some uncontroversial sense, Salman's mind. They'll agree too, about exactly how we've got to this position. So the puzzle about whether it's Salman or Hanif eating breakfast isn't really a puzzle as to what the facts are — it's just a puzzle as to what's the best, the most natural, or most appropriate thing to say. But disagreement here is merely verbal, and there just might not be a best, most natural response. And the real case. Some thought that with his mind and memory gone, Ronald Reagan was no longer with us. For others, so long as there was life, the former president still existed. But again, there isn't any genuine disagreement here, no discovery we might make, or imagine we might make, that would settle the question either way. Again, the puzzle, if there is one, is just about what will seem to us the best thing to say.

Chapter Eight

Is It All Meaningless?

One day I had Bertrand Russell in the cab. So I said to him, 'Well, then, Lord Russell, what's it all about?' And, do you know, he couldn't tell me.
(London taxi driver)

'Life is meaningless' is itself meaningless. Think about the sorts of things that might have, or might lack, meaning – words, sentences, road signs, icons on the laptop, squiggles that tell you what to do with the washing machine. Other things, such as cats, daffodils, asteroid belts, and life itself are quite different, and though much can be said about them, they're neither meaningful nor meaningless. So this whole question about the meaning of life rests on a mistake. And it takes a halfway decent philosopher five minutes or less to sort it out.

Well, that's one approach, the kind of brisk, tweedy, somewhat complacent attitude that, especially in Britain, and around the middle of the last century, got philosophy a bad name. It's neither as impressive nor as convincing as it likes to think. People who wonder about the meaning of life aren't making a simple mistake, asking what 'life' stands for (as with signs and symbols), or how to translate it (as with sentences in a foreign language). And only rarely can they be fobbed off with the suggestion that even in asking about meaning, they reveal themselves as thoroughly confused.

Yet, if not confused, what is it, exactly, that we are after? Those of us who are troubled about the meaning of life are puzzling about the sense, the point, the purpose, the significance of it all. If it's meaningless, then it's senseless, purposeless, with no real value or worth in anything we do, and no good reason, in the end, ever to get out of bed. We can think this in different ways. For some people the idea that there is no meaning is directed just to their own lives – it's of personal, local, and often temporary concern – while for others it seems that all lives are, and indeed must be, lacking in meaning and point, whether people recognize this or not. And while some are deeply depressed, perhaps incapacitated, by the thought that life is meaningless, others grit their teeth and continue with their day-to-day existence. Still others find the idea strangely liberating – life without meaning is life in which we float free, unrestrained, in charge of our own destiny.

Is life meaningless? It's a question that many of us, at some time or other, worry about. And it's probably this question, more than any other, that people think philosophers should be concerned with. If lovers of wisdom can't sort this one, then heaven help us.

Why Think Life is Meaningless?

What drives the thought that there is no meaning in life? What is it that makes us feel that, ultimately, life has neither purpose nor point? For now, think big.

One thought is about the inescapable brevity of life – we know full well that we'll soon be gone, forgotten, exiting the universe with scarce a trace left behind. And this isn't a point just about individuals. Not only will each of us die, but in the longer run our species, like all others, will become extinct, and in the longer run still nothing that any of us has done, building pyramids, writing plays, sending rockets into deepest space, will leave any tangible remains. Dust to dust, but in the end even the dust will be gone.

Another, and related, thought is that even now we, our works, and our world are altogether minuscule in comparison with the vastness of the cosmos. Look at the night sky, think of the countless galaxies, stars, planets that it contains, and our whole existence pales into insignificance. Remember that bit in *The Third Man* where the Orson Welles character, lording it from high on the Ferris wheel, likens the people below him to ants. From any position that we in fact occupy, this seems a bit harsh, but take an imaginary view from the centre of the universe, and our lives and endeavours will seem much less than ant-like; nothing more than the faintest of scurryings in one little corner of the Milky Way.

A third thought is that our condition here is far from enviable – life, for all of us, is a constant series of struggles, setback after setback, in which pain, frustration, disappointment, loss is, if we face up to things, quite clearly all we can expect. Of course, we tell ourselves that life can be good, that pleasure, happiness, success are just around the corner, but we're pulling the wool over our eyes, and refusing to see things as really they are. Schopenhauer, philosophy's prime pessimist, has this as his abiding theme:

We begin in the madness of carnal desire and the transport of voluptuousness, we end in the dissolution of all our parts, and the musty stench of corpses. And the road from the one to the other too goes, in regard to our well-being and the enjoyment of life, steadily downhill: happily dreaming childhood, exultant youth, toil-filled years of manhood, infirm and often wretched old age, the torment of the last illness and finally the throes of death – does it not look as if existence were an error, the consequences of which gradually grow more and more manifest?

A gloomy picture, undoubtedly, but it's hard to deny that it contains something of the truth.

A final thought here is, for many people, a major reason for admitting that life has neither purpose nor point. This is the atheist's idea that there is, after all, no God, no creator, no one looking after us, or fitting us into his scheme. And without God, without a master plan, it's just of no consequence, ultimately, what we do, or whether we live or die. This idea, that we stand alone, unwanted and unplanned, fits, of course, with other things. No God, and no guarantee of our future importance. No God, and only a peripheral place in the order of things. No God, and no goodness, no justice, here on Earth. Anything goes, and nothing matters. It isn't the only issue, but for many the suspicion that the claims of religion don't stand up is of central importance in arguments for the meaninglessness of life.

Thus, on one or other of several counts, it may well seem that life is utterly devoid of meaning. Temporary, marginal, adrift within an indifferent and uncaring universe, we so easily might not have existed. And while so many things continue so much to occupy us, we can surely see, if we think it through, that in reality none of it matters a jot.

Are These Reasons Any Good?

Yet before putting an end to it all, before giving up in despair, we need to ask whether these reasons are any good. Do they really work as the pessimists among us suggest, showing that life is without point or purpose? Or is there something fishy going on?

One way to resist these arguments is to challenge, from the outset, their accounts of life, the universe and everything. Perhaps this is easiest when faced with Schopenhauer's miserable view of our current lot. Many of us will think that life isn't as bad as he pictures it, and that while pain, frustration and the rest are not to be denied, they don't give us the whole story, and not even the main story about many of our lives. There are genuine satisfactions, genuine pleasures to be had. And even though we all die in the end, and often sooner than we'd like, this neither undoes all that happens on the way, nor suggests that the journey itself goes steadily downhill. Lots of people are going to object, similarly, to the last of the points above. For even if it's hard to prove anything for certain either way, lots of people do believe, of course, that God exists, and do believe that our existence does, in religious terms, serve some purpose, some point. And if the argument against God is flawed, so too is the argument against meaning.

It's going to be harder to counter the other arguments, though. Much of what science tells us about the history and vastness of the universe is pretty much established fact. Maybe you can imagine that vestiges of our existence will somehow last throughout time; maybe you can even imagine that we might succeed in colonizing some parts of outer space, giving human beings a chance to continue even when our solar system is gone, but it seems unlikely. It seems even more unlikely that scientists have things wrong about the size of the universe, and that it might turn out that human beings do, after all, loom large and centrally within in. And so if facts like these can rob our lives of meaning, it will seem that our existence is pointless after all.

But can they? A second approach is to question whether these alleged facts are really as important as is sometimes assumed. Take first the point about size. Agreed, the universe is big, and we are small; but why should that matter? And if you think it does matter, then just imagine that things are different. For if being small is such a problem, then surely we'd be better off if we were, relatively speaking, a bigger deal. So imagine that large parts of the universe have never existed, and that the facts are much as they were long thought to be – Earth at the centre, sun, moon and planets orbiting around us, and the starry firmament beyond. And then ask, would this help restore meaning to our lives? It's hard to see how it would. For it's hard to see how the existence or non-existence of stars or planets billions of miles away can make any difference to the meaning or significance of things happening here.

Similarly for time. Why should it matter that we'll all be gone in a million years? That's a long way down the line. Again, one way to test whether this matters is to imagine that things are different, and that in fact we will go on, avoiding extinction, and avoiding dust. So suppose that there is some guarantee that human beings will continue forever, talking about the weather, doing up their houses, fussing about their looks, making, alternately, love and war. Even if you think of this as good news, you might still wonder how it helps. So, life will go on for ever and ever. How can any of us feel our own lives will have more point, more significance because of changes as large, but also as distant, and as detached, as this? Isn't it just irrelevant to the question of meaning now?

The same approach can be used with some of the fears about atheism, and its alleged consequences for meaning. And so used, it reveals something important about different kinds of meaning, and the kind we want for our lives. Imagine or suppose, then, that there is a God, a heaven and a hell, that he wants the good to flourish and the evil to suffer, and plans, for the righteous among us, everlasting communion with him. Again, we might wonder whether this really helps. So we are to live forever, to do as God wills, and then, unceasingly, to praise him. That might sound a lot better than some of the alternatives, and it's surely much, much better than hell, but are worries about the meaninglessness, the pointlessness of our lives really going to be settled in this way? Are we really going to be satisfied by finding that we fit into someone else's grand scheme? There's some sort of meaning and purpose in this, but is it the sort we want? Imagine something like Shakespeare's *The Tempest*, with people stuck on a desert island, not really knowing why they're there or what they're supposed to do, drifting aimlessly. Then they discover that they're a part of some psychological experiment, and everything they do is noted down and fed into computers by men in white coats. Why should this make them feel any better? Or imagine turkeys thinking their lives are meaningless, and then in the end discovering that their point is to get fat for, and give pleasure at, Christmas. Unless the turkeys are really stupid, this won't come as good news.

What this shows, I think, is that what we're after is not just any old meaning and purpose, but meaning and purpose that we can find for ourselves, or at least that we can ourselves identify with, and commit to. And it's this that once we start to think about it seems so elusive, seems constantly to slip between our fingers. It's easy enough for things to have a purpose or point for someone else – dishwashers, clocks, lawnmowers have point and purpose for us, and we can, as above, imagine that we, in turn, serve someone else's purpose. But we don't want to be like this. We don't want simply to fit into another's scheme. But then nor do we want to be pointless, gratuitous, things that don't matter at all. What we want is to find our own purposes, making or discovering for ourselves life's meaning.

Where does this leave us? Some of the standard arguments for life having no meaning turn out to be less effective than they first seemed. But we shouldn't take too much comfort from this. Even if these arguments don't work, others perhaps might. And what became clearer at the end of the paragraph above, that we need, not someone else's meaning, but meaning of our own, might present obstacles that are not at all easy to overcome.

Lives and Meanings

Maybe, though, this is all too grand. And maybe we go wrong in looking at things on such a cosmic scale. Maybe, too, we get off to a bad start by asking the wrong question. Put it this way – 'What is the meaning of life?' – and we're set looking for the one simple thing that works in every case to give our lives their point. But then the search for this magical ingredient is so certain to fail, that we'll end up simply joking about it, suggesting, as in *The Hitchhiker's Guide to the Galaxy*, that the meaning of life is 42, or sitting through old *Monty Python* sketches, where men dressed up as women are looking out for the thing that the meaning is.

Better, then, to tweak the question in two respects. First, instead of thinking of life in general, or, in some abstract fashion, of the human condition, think of individual human lives. And then ask which of these lives, if any, are meaningful, and which are not. Second, instead of thinking of the one thing that will give a life its meaning, and then thinking of that one thing in all or nothing terms, think instead of the various things that might to various degrees help make a life more or less meaningful. Think like this, think smaller, in piecemeal and local terms, and maybe we'll get somewhere.

It's Up to You

Here's one suggestion. Whether or not your life is meaningful is up to you. There are no rules about such things. And certainly no one else is in a position to judge. It just depends how you feel about it – if you feel your life is meaningful, then it is; if you feel it's not, then it isn't. Questions about the meaning of life, then, are, to use a familiar term, altogether subjective.

It's a suggestion, but is it a good one? Think about the following case, obviously invented, but not a million miles from real ones:

Chrysanthemum Chorus. Angelica is an ambitious gardener. Highly ambitious. Not only does she want her lawn to be greener and stripier than any in her town, not only is she after cherries, lemons and apricots in a climate where others are happy enough with runner beans, but she's set on the most impressive flowers anywhere. And not simply in terms of their looks or their scent, or how long they last. She wants them to sing. There's a limit to her ambition, so she's not working on them all at once. For now she's concentrating on the chrysanthemums, erect, uniform, big heads, altogether impressive. She talks to them, plays them music, stands before them with her baton. If there's any singing to be had these, she's sure, are her best bet.

Is Angelica leading a meaningful life? She's certainly busy, and in spite of the inevitable setbacks, she remains cheerful. Maybe she's even happy. But is life spent in this way a life of meaning? Or is it a complete waste of time? Is she, as you might suspect, simply mad?

Maybe it isn't, and never will be, perfectly clear what we're after, when we're after a meaningful life, but it seems to me that Angelica has lost the plot on this one. Certainly some things are up to us, or subjective, and if we sincerely believe them, then they are. Suppose she's got a headache. The doctor might say there's nothing physiologically wrong, but if she believes she's in pain, then she is. And this is why I allow that she's cheerful. She's the best judge of that. Maybe – though this is more controversial – people are the best judges also of whether or not they're happy. Maybe if you think you're happy, then you are. But some things are certainly not up to us. Is Angelica leading a successful life? Suppose we ask her. And – an important point – we ask her what this success consists in. Important, because it just doesn't make sense to claim success without any reasons. Perhaps she says her life's a success because she is, or is about to be, the world's first leader of a fully trained chrysanthemum choir. Well, she's not. If she thinks her life a success for these reasons, she's simply wrong. Perhaps she thinks she's advancing scientific knowledge. It seems unlikely that she is. But the important point is that this too is a claim about how things stand outside of Angelica's head – it doesn't become true just because she thinks it is. Whether or not your life is successful depends on how it matches up against certain external criteria – it doesn't depend simply on how you feel about it. And I think it's the same for whether your life is meaningful. Here, too, thinking doesn't make it so. And Angelica is, I would suggest, living a foolish, pointless existence, in pursuit of a ridiculous – and pretty obviously ridiculous – dream.

Is it acceptable, though, simply to trot out such harsh and unyielding verdicts on the way people go about their lives? Shouldn't we live and let live, respecting the choices that others make? Some people will worry about the sort of approach adopted here, finding it too judgemental. After all, Angelica's not doing anyone any harm. And she seems happy enough. Think, though, about more realistic cases. Someone you know gets through university, settles down, lands a good job, but then develops a drug habit. And things begin to collapse. Family and friends try to intervene, to get him back on the straight and narrow. But why? He, too, is doing no one any harm. Imagine his parents are rich enough to support him, so he isn't on the road to crime. He isn't in pain or suffering in any obvious way. Indeed he might appear happier than the rest of us. But the objection to such a life is simply that it seems a waste, a missed opportunity, a pointless existence. Perhaps to say this is, indeed, to be judgemental. But then it doesn't seem as if being judgemental is something we need always to avoid.

Getting It Right

We shouldn't think, then, that anything goes. Perhaps we do have to find or make for ourselves meaning in our lives. But we can't find it just anywhere, and we can't make it up as we go along. It isn't, whatever people say, all subjective. That approach won't work. But now if there are objective criteria – things we can agree or disagree about, things that eventually we might settle on – as to what makes a life more or less meaningful, what indeed are they? What do we need, in order for our lives to have meaning?

This is where things may become deeply disappointing. And that's because the suggestions I'm going to make here are none of them very exciting or particularly profound. They're just familiar, everyday suggestions about what makes a life meaningful, significant, or worth living. And they've all been mentioned before, by philosophers, novelists, priests, healers, and others besides.

Here, then, are some of the things that matter – relationships, pursuing some plan or project, living a good life. These are the sorts of things that sit, often, towards the centre of the meaningful life. It's looking like a short list, but unpacking the items here will, I think, prove worthwhile.

First, then, relationships with other people, with friends, family, children is, or so I'm suggesting, one of the important elements that helps to make a life meaningful. Suppose you are involved with others in this way. You share in their aspirations, hope things go well for them, take pleasure in their pleasures. And at the same time you enjoy their company, open up to them with some of your own problems and concerns, get their help when it's needed. It isn't easy, in recognizing this, altogether to doubt whether your life is of any significance, or value or point. And the significance or point here seems to be of the right kind – friends need each quite differently from the way we need postmen or farmers or people in call centres in Scotland or Bangalore. Good relationships are reciprocal, and there is the feeling on neither side of being used, valued for one thing alone, or merely fitted in to another's scheme. Silas Marner, in George Eliot's novel, discovers profound meaning in his life when he comes across, and decides to raise as his own, a baby girl left on his doorstep. And conversely, the hero, or anti-hero, in the John Wayne film *The Searchers* has his life drained of meaning when his entire family is massacred by Indians. I'm thinking, obviously, of other people here, but, even if they can never be more than second best, it has to be allowed that relationships with pets – cats and dogs most notably – can similarly help invest our lives with meaning.

And then, second, commitment to some plan, or project, or scheme. Suppose you have some big and driving idea, maybe to write a novel, visit the capitals of Europe, restore a Victorian house, or grow your own vegetables and learn to cook them. You read up on the subject, organize your money and your time, work out your plan of campaign, get involved with and then get pleasure out of its realisation. Again, commitment to any such scheme sits uncomfortably with the thought that your life is meaningless, utterly without purpose or point. And again, there are examples from literature that illustrate this – the narrator in Proust's novel, like Proust himself, finds that his shapeless and often misdirected life comes together, acquiring meaning and point, when he is able to step back, detail its progress, and transmute it into art.

Third, something more controversial. I'm not sure that this is right, but it's a widespread idea, and certainly needs mention. Think of what being a good person involves – awareness of the some of the ills of the world, and a strong desire to change things for the better. It involves too, and probably first, an ordering of things within – a good person is someone who has a grip on life, a sense of proportion, of what matters, a proper way to balance competing concerns. Get the sense, get the balance and then focus at least a part of your energies on righting wrongs elsewhere. And if this is right, and self-help and helping others should in this way be linked, then it seem likely that the morally good life will be at the same time a meaningful life.

These different points are all of them connected. Involvement with others will often give rise to some sort of plan or project – maybe to help your kids get through school and university, or working with friends to put on plays or concerts in the village hall. Living a moral life, in its familiar sense, is highly likely to involve you with other people. Many plans and projects will again do this, either because you need others to help work things through, or because there's a natural tendency to share enthusiasms with like-minded people. And then what at a deeper level knits these various activities together seems to be, first, an awareness of the temporal dimension to our lives, awareness that we're not simply living from moment to moment, and, second, a concern to give these lives an articulation and coherence, and to do this, often, by creatively shaping and structuring things elsewhere. The meaningful life, then, is often self-conscious, future-directed, and constructive.

I need to come back to religion here. The suggestion earlier was that the death of God isn't going to strip our lives of meaning. And the further, and connected, suggestion was that God's existence, even if it gives our lives meaning of a sort, won't really do it for the kind of meaning we want. But I don't at all want to suggest that religion is simply irrelevant, besides the point, where the meaning of life is concerned. First, if religion turns out to be true, it may be that we'll discover, in the end, that there is an overall shape or pattern to life, not one that is imposed on us from outside, but one that we can understand, acknowledge, and take up as our own. God's ways might, in the end, be revealed as the ways we would have chosen for ourselves. Second, and here more important, even supposing that there is no God, those who believe in him and live the religious life, might well, because of these beliefs, live a life of meaning. For, certainly, religion does get us to focus on the bigger picture, the longer term, turning from narrow, self-centred and often trivial concerns to a larger community of more pressing needs. Religious belief, then, even if in the end there's nothing in it, will encourage involvement with the kinds of things – concern with others, with the future, with amelioration – which, or so I've suggested, will help give our lives significance and meaning.

All of this, and intentionally, is somewhat loose and vague. I'm suggesting only that the kinds of things here discussed can help to give meaning to your life. I don't say you need them all – a hermit, for example, might well lead a meaningful life, as too could someone not much given to the good. And even if religion can help, it is, I think, far from necessary. For even if you agree that we need to acknowledge the spiritual dimension to life, it is a mistake, surely, to think religion alone can allow us to do that. I don't say, either, that if you have all these things in your life, then meaning is somehow guaranteed. In a number of different ways it might still be compromised.

Getting It Wrong

What, then, stands in the way of meaning? If the sorts of things mentioned above can contribute to the meaningful life, what, in contrast, will detract from it? I can start here with, again, some straightforward and familiar points, and then go on to suggest certain refinements.

First, further features in our lives, when present to any significant degree, can work against life having meaning. Pain, illness, whether physical or psychological, extreme poverty can all drain life of its significance and point. Again, these are near truisms – it's hard to be involved with others, to keep up your flute practice, or to put the world to rights if you're spending all the hours of the day thinking about pain and how to be rid of it, or where you can possibly get something to eat or drink. Not everyone is in the condition that Schopenhauer describes, but for those who are, it's a bad way to be. Again, there's no suggestion that we can work to a rule book on these things. People can live meaningful lives in spite of pain. Moreover, pain and suffering can in some circumstances help to give life meaning. Since he was shot, paralysed, and confined to a wheelchair, the American pornographer Larry Flynt has, on his own account, found that his life has changed for the better. The point is just that, very often, the bad things in life do threaten its meaning, significance, and purpose.

Second, the absence, entirely, of those things mentioned above, will undermine the claim to meaning. Someone cut off from other people, unable, for whatever reason, to fully engage with any long-term project, prevented from making any positive difference to the world, is unlikely to find meaning in life. Imagine Robinson Crusoe, without Friday, no hope of escape, and on an island where the food is so plentiful he doesn't even have to scheme to stay alive. Nothing happens. And it seems to him there's no importance to anything he does. Or think of the kinds of lives on offer in Aldous Huxley's *Brave New World*, with its vision of an antiseptic and cosseted future, in which little of what we can do has any deeper purpose or value. On a more mundane level, lose your job, and your friends, and your life may well seem without meaning or point.

Third, it's going to be important not to pursue even the positive things to excess. That's another way of getting things wrong. Think of someone who is always busy with her family or friends, who seems to live through them, who is never at ease with herself. Think, again, of the saint, forever looking for the moral angle, always unwilling to let rip. Such a person may indeed be living, in one sense, a good life, and may well do a lot of good for others. But we might wonder whether this is a good life in the further sense, and whether someone who is so thoroughly self-abnegating can be said to live a meaningful existence. Or think of someone totally wrapped up in some project. Writers, painters, musicians are often driven, obsessive, monomaniacal figures, unable ever to stem their creative juices. Even if their works make our lives richer and deeper, we should be careful, I think, not to assume that they themselves are similarly rewarded. So don't think the meaningful life is the prerogative of only the few – Beethoven, Gandhi, Napoleon, Einstein. Think instead that such a life is much more widely available, and that you and I might have a better chance of it than giants and heroes.

Some Complications

All of this may seem suspiciously straightforward. But now some of these points need to be revisited, with complications explored, and worries allayed.

Go back, first, to the point about morality. I want to say that while the good life might well help with meaning, it isn't altogether necessary. We don't know that Shakespeare, or Catherine the Great, or Thomas Edison were particularly good people, yet it seems they lead meaningful lives. But what about the bad person? Hitler, Stalin, Pol Pot had plans and projects which in large part they realized, as too, on a smaller though still significant scale, did Jack the Ripper and Al Capone. Should we say that their lives were meaningful? Some philosophers have thought that meaning and morality are quite clearly distinct – what matters is the involvement with some project, and not its ethical dimension. But there's room for doubt. Just as we might think that madness is a handicap to meaning, so too for badness. If we think of these characters as not simply misinformed, but positively evil, then it seems we can wonder how they can really believe their lives are worthwhile. If, as many insist, evil eats at the soul, then the chances of a thoroughly bad person leading a meaningful life would appear to be slim.

And did I really get it right about Angelica? She has a plan, a project, something she's committed to, that gives shape and structure to her life. Why isn't it meaningful? It's a good question. But I think an idea that most of us share is that not any old project will do — it has to be both feasible and worthwhile. Or, if not that, at least it should seem to reasonable people to be feasible and worthwhile. No one was ever going to discover phlogiston, but from the perspective of what was known at the time, it wasn't crazy to try. Yet some projects are crazy, and only a mad person can think they've any chance of success. You can't jump to the moon. Others, though achievable, are pointless. You could count the leaves on an avenue of trees, or make a note of whenever clouds appear or disappear, but without some further aim in mind, these are very silly things to do.

A related worry: is engagement really necessary? Angelica is involved in a project which, I've said, is silly, futile, pointless. But what about the opposite case?

> *Nine to Five.* Jean-Paul has worked for the International Red Cross for most of his adult life. He's an administrator, a key player in managing the response to famine, earthquake, war wherever they occur. He was born in Algeria, and from childhood on made aware — his parents were communists — that colonialism, imperialism, has its darker sides. It seemed inevitable that he would in some ways follow in their wake, concerned for social justice, and helping those most in need. But over the years his passion has worn thin. Even though he's good, indeed very good, at what he does, Jean-Paul thinks of it now as a job of work, something for the office, and that efficiency counts for more than enthusiasm.

Some people will think of this as a meaningful life, even if Jean-Paul himself is no longer particularly committed to what he is doing. I'm not so sure. It's been a valuable life in obvious ways — the projects he works on are undoubtedly worthwhile, with thousands of people owing everything to his efforts — but Jean-Paul remains curiously detached from his work, and doesn't think that it enriches or enhances his own existence. He is perhaps like Oskar Schindler, whose helping Jews to escape from the Nazis appears not to have figured in the detailed weave of his life.

This helps clear up another point. It was insisted earlier that your life isn't meaningful simply because you believe it to be so. But the suggestion now is that attitudes do matter, and that a lack of engagement can threaten or subvert meaning. This isn't at all inconsistent. We can say that attitudes aren't the be-all and end-all, even though they help. (Think of other cases. You don't become attractive to other people, or good fun at parties, or a star of the debating chamber simply by thinking you are. But having a positive attitude will certainly increase your chances.) So a better position stresses the two sides to the story, giving attention both to the kind of life we lead, and our attitudes towards that life. As one recent philosopher has put it: 'Meaning arises when subjective attraction meets objective attractiveness.' And this seems right.

A final worry involves a deeper and more difficult question. What I've said, with certain qualifications, is that some kinds of lives will seem to us to be meaningful, while others will strike us as much less so. But is this good enough? Even if we agree about what counts, what matters, couldn't it still be that we have it wrong? Couldn't we all be systematically in error about which are the more, which the less, meaningful lives?

I don't think so. Certainly there are lots of mistakes we could make. We might, for example, have completely the wrong end of the stick about the bottom of the sea, or the long-term effects of genetic engineering. But while science contains many obstacles to understand, the meaning of life, as I've been talking about it in the sections above, is a matter curiously close to our hearts, with several complications, but few hidden depths. It's not at all easy to see how, if we think carefully and collectively about it, we could altogether miss the point.

Meaning and Absurdity

And yet a sense of unease will remain. What started out as a deep worry about the ultimate incoherence and pointlessness of our lives has been side-tracked into a series of near platitudinous observations about the sorts of things that just might make one life slightly better, in the meaning stakes, than another. But why shouldn't we admit that even while there are these real differences between lives, they are nevertheless all lacking in genuine meaning? It's true that on a day to day basis we are, usually, fully occupied with living our lives – it seems incredibly important that we get to some meeting on time, or do better in the next squash game than the last, or find the right tiles to decorate the kitchen. But then later, looking back, these things turn out to matter hardly at all, so much so that it can be embarrassing to recollect how wrapped up in them we were at the time. And even if from within our lives the point and purpose of what we do may seem obvious — and a headache does, after all, give you good reason to take an aspirin — we can't help but suspect, if we step back, that, in the end, none of it counts. Ultimately, it seems, there is neither meaning nor significance in anything we do.

Here though, it is important to be philosophical. But I don't mean this in the popular sense, that we should be accepting of our lot, resigned and stoical about it all. Rather, what's important is to take great care with some very ordinary bits of language.

Does it really matter that you get to that meeting on time? The world won't end if you miss it. And even it did, the universe would still go on. But something can matter, and matter a lot, even when the consequences are far less grand. It does matter a lot that people don't die in their thousands in genocidal wars, even if, either way, the world and the universe will go on. Does something that matters a lot really matter? You might want to agonize over that, but I'd suggest that 'really' isn't doing any genuine work here. Mattering, and really mattering, are not two different things. And it's the same with the word 'just'. This can similarly deceive us into thinking it makes a genuine difference to sentences in which it appears. We might say that we are just tiny, freakish creatures held in a moment of time. But 'just' here merely gestures towards potency and weight. Elsewhere, though, 'just' works differently. Some people have looked at the lives of insects — glow-worms, mayflies, crickets — and suggested that our lives are just like theirs — an endless cycle of birth, copulation, and death. If we were just like insects, then our lives would be as lacking in meaning as are theirs. But it seems quite unwarranted to assume that the differences here — self-consciousness, an emotional life, this constant questioning — count for nothing. Our lives, then, are not, in truth, just like theirs.

And what of ultimately mattering? This term is less ambiguous than 'real'. And we should perhaps simply agree that ultimately, our existence doesn't matter at all. But this isn't just one of those things, an absence that might be remedied by hard work or invention. Nor is it a deep and unavoidable tragedy, something that might, quite reasonably, cause us from time to time to stop and shudder. For, first, there is nothing we can so much as imagine that would put ultimate meaning in our lives — it's absolutely impossible that there should be such a thing. And, second, while some things that are impossible yet seem to make a bit of sense, and seem still to be things you might want — time travel is perhaps like this — others, when you think hard about them, show up as altogether incoherent. And the notion of ultimate meaning looks to be like this. We feel ourselves close up against the utter fortuitousness of our existence. And life seems pointless. But it can't be enough to fit into a grander scheme – to be at the centre of the universe, to be the children of God. It might be good if some such were true. But still we could ask what lies behind all this. What is the point of the divine plan, within which we have a point? Even God isn't ultimate enough, on the meaning front, to put these worries to rest. And that being so, we should conclude, I think, that such worries are simply not real.

Maybe this still isn't satisfying. And the American philosopher Thomas Nagel has had another go at it, arguing that because such worries will keep coming back to us, we ought to conclude that life is absurd. This isn't quite the same thing as saying that it's meaningless. Remember the concerns with which we started out – nothing lasts forever, God is dead, we are small, and so, because of all this, meaning is gone. Nagel agrees that these arguments don't really work. We still have all our short- and medium-term meanings, purpose and point on the local scale. And what more, really, can we ask for? But then Nagel thinks this isn't the end of the story either, and that what we do, and what really we can't help doing, is oscillate between the two perspectives or viewpoints on the world. So while we often see life from here, from inside, and are then engaged with, and committed to it, we not infrequently step back and view our lives as from afar, as if looking down on ourselves from some outside and distant point. When engaged, life seems to us to be meaningful; when we step back, meaning simply disappears. And because this switching back and forth between the two perspectives, unable finally to settle on either one, is a part of the human condition; because life can on the same day, within the same hour, seem to us to be both deadly serious and a killing joke, so it is, for Nagel, right to think it absurd. And how to respond to that? Don't make a fuss. Don't think, along with Albert Camus, that suicide is the only decent response, but take it in your stride.

Is life absurd? Nagel's argument is clever, and has been enormously influential, but I don't think it's successful. And that's because I'm not persuaded by this irreconcilable clash of perspectives. Certainly we can make mistakes. We can think on the one day that nothing is more important than that we find the right shirt to go with these shoes, and then on the next that nothing we do is of the slightest consequence. But both these thoughts are wrong. Getting the right shirt, even if it is important, is never of the utmost importance. And many things are of consequence, even if they make only marginal differences to the history of the universe. These thoughts are both true, and so consistent with one another, and so, in turn, undermining of any stubborn clash of perspectives. And so the case for absurdity disappears.

Does Meaning Matter?

It might seem obvious that this concern with the meaning of life is well judged, something that we ought to take seriously, and think about for some time. Certainly, many of us will take for granted that this is so. And perhaps it had better be so, if it's to deserve a place among my good questions. But there's a related question, itself worth asking, about whether we should be as bothered as we are to make our lives meaningful.

One thing to notice is that these questions about meaning are, in some measure, of merely local concern. Not all people in all periods have fussed about it the way we do today. It isn't something they go on about in Jane Austen, for example, or in eighteenth century theatre, and it doesn't feature as a dominant theme for either side in the English Civil War. Shakespeare seems likely to have worried about it, with, for example, Macbeth thinking of life as 'a tale told by an idiot, full of sound and fury, signifying nothing' as did his near contemporary Rabelais, in France, whose last words were, allegedly 'Ring down the curtain, the farce is over.' Euripedes, about the last of the great playwrights of ancient Greece, had it as a theme as well, with many of his characters raging against the arbitrariness and futility of their existence. And, as various writings by Schopenhauer and Tolstoy, Chekhov and Nietzsche all indicate, it's certainly something of an issue in the mid- to late-nineteenth century. What seems to be suggested, taking all this into account, is that a concern with meaning often surfaces in times of religious doubt, and affects especially those who find their assumptions about meaning through God or gods are coming under threat.

What, then, about the present? Again, it's worth trying to see things in context. And it seems as if much of our current concern with meaning can be traced back, first, to French existentialists – most notably to Camus, but also to Sartre and Beckett, and second to the spread of existentialism in America in the 1960s and the 1970s. So dig beneath the surface, and an issue that might at first seem to be one of the perennials of philosophy can appear instead to be closely linked with beatniks, drop-outs, and the forbiddingly self-indulgent navel-gazing of the so-called me generation.

Still, nothing much follows from that. Even if we find that there is something intermittent about attempts to give answers; in some ages people may have been too complacent to ask, while in others the need to tackle the basics – getting food and shelter, avoiding disease and war – has stood in the way; it may still be that the question itself should be of ongoing concern. Perhaps there's a sense in which a life of meaning is the birthright of us all.

Yet there is room for doubt. Is it really that important to live a meaningful life? Consider this example:

> *The Smallholding.* Massimo inherited the land from his father, between the wars. He'll leave it in turn to his eldest son, Giulio. The soil isn't that good, but there's an olive grove, a fair-sized vegetable patch – his wife mainly looks after this, she was from the next village, further towards the Puglian coast, from a family known for hard work and breeding boys – and high pasture for the sheep. Not much changes – gestures towards land reform, that interval with the fascists, something about a common market – and so far as he can, Massimo keeps his head down. What he wants is for the olives to ripen, food on the table, evenings in the square with the other men, a glass of wine, a game of chess.

It's a life. But it isn't, at least according to the criteria suggested, a particularly meaningful life. Massimo lives, more or less, from day to day, or at least from season to season. He's no particular plans or projects that excite him, he's not an especially good person, and though his family and the men he drinks with matter to him, they don't, to be honest, matter all that much. But nor is it a meaningless life. Neither setbacks nor frustrations dog his days, and neither illness nor disease loom large for him or for those he cares about. Nor does Massimo himself think of his life as either meaningful or meaningless. It's a life, good enough, and better, surely, than many. So why not leave it at that?

That a life might be neither meaningful nor meaningless has already been implied, in the suggestion that meaning is a matter of degree. Unsurprisingly, many will fall within the no man's land between the two. But is that such a bad thing? Are lives better the more full of meaning they are? It might be assumed that they are, but it's worth considering whether this is really so. Nagel, in his arguments about the absurd, points out that a mouse's life is neither meaningful nor meaningless – mice, and animals in general, are not able to stand back, muse on life, and wonder about its purpose or point. But it should be remembered that we are animals too, and even if we are given, often, to reflection, it might be a useful part of that reflective practice to wonder, from time to time, whether so much reflection is really such a good thing.

I set Massimo in country, with his animals, trees and garden, partly because this sort of day-to-day routine, following the rhythms of the seasons, close to nature and the soil, has seemed, so often, to offer an altogether appropriate, balanced and sane kind of existence, even if not one of particular profundity or meaning. It's the sort of life that appealed to Tolstoy, in his later years, when he wanted so much to identify with the peasants on his estate. It appeals too, to many in Chekhov's plays, driven to distraction by the boredom and emptiness of their bourgeois existence. Wittgenstein worked in a monastery garden when, soon after the First World War, he was looking for some respite from the exhaustions of philosophy. And after their whirlwind, worldwide and altogether wearying adventures, it's to just such a safe house that Voltaire's characters turn at the end of *Candide*.

'I also know', said Candide, 'that we must go and work in the garden.'

'You are quite right', said Pangloss. 'When man was placed in the Garden of Eden, he was put there "to dress it and to keep it", to work, in fact; which proves that man was not born to an easy life.'

'We must work without arguing', said Martin; 'that is the only way to make life bearable.'

The entire household agreed to this admirable plan, and each began to exercise his talents. Small as the estate was, it bore heavy crops. There was no denying that Cunegonde was decidedly ugly, but she soon made excellent pastry. Pacquette was excellent at embroidery, and the old woman took care of the linen. No one refused to work, not even Brother Giroflée, who was a good carpenter, and thus became an honest man. From time to time Pangloss would say to Candide:

'There is a chain of events in this best of all possible worlds; for if you had not been turned out of a beautiful mansion at the point of a jackboot for the love of Lady Cunegonde, and if you had not been involved in the Inquisition, and had not wandered over America on foot, and had not struck the Baron with your sword, and lost all those sheep you brought from El Dorado, you would not be here eating candied fruit and pistachio nuts.'

'That's true enough,' said Candide; 'but we must go and work in the garden.'

Is It All Meaningless?

Because there are different questions about meaning, there will, unsurprisingly, be different answers. Think about the local question, think about different lives, and it seems that some will be meaningful, and others meaningless. As I've said, we're talking differences of degree here, so perhaps only a few will be at either end of the scale, with most falling somewhere or other between. And whether lives are meaningful in this way will depend both on what they're like, and also on what we think about them. Get the right attitude to the right life, and things will start to look good, so far as meaning is concerned.

Yet there is also as well the global question, that of whether any of our lives, or the existence of our species, or the universe itself has any ultimate or real meaning or point. I've wanted to say the answer here is no. But I've wanted to say, also, that this isn't something we should get too depressed about. For we can't even imagine what could provide for meaning on this global scale. So its absence isn't the lack of anything real.

Does this mean we shouldn't worry about meaning? Some people, I've suggested, don't, and are happy enough just to live their lives. That's alright. Others do. They look up into the night sky, or reflect on the disasters of war, or marvel at the variety of human endeavour, and wonder what it's all about. Even if we decide that we can see that, really, there is nothing that it's all about, that's alright as well.

Chapter Nine

Should There Be More, and Better, People?

The ultimate economic betterment should be sought by breeding better people, not fewer of the existing sort.
(The Eugenic Record Office, 1910)

One good question concerns the number of people who are born. Are there as many as there should be? A lot of people think there's no right answer to this question. But others think there are clearly too few. For they think that, other things equal, the more people there are, the better it is. Another good question is about the sorts of people who are born. Are they, or their lives, as good as they should be? Only a few think there's no right answer here. Most think that the better lives are, the better it is.

These two questions, the first about the number of lives, the second about their quality, can look to be quite different from one another. But I think they're connected. And I think, as well, that in both cases we should offer negative answers. It isn't better if more lives are lived. And it isn't better, either, if better lives are lived. There are certain complications, as I'll explain below, in talking about the quality of lives. It's a bit easier to deal with numbers. So that's a place to start.

More People

The world's population hit six billion some time in 1999. Some of us think this is more than enough, and point to overcrowding in Mexico and Bangladesh, the damage we do to the environment, and pressure on resources – oil, water, rainforests – that are necessary to our lives. It would be good, then, if our numbers could be substantially reduced. Others say there could be billions more, and that we could use empty space in

Canada, Mongolia, Scotland, to build new cities and expand the world population still further. We could argue about the practicalities here, and about whether there's really overcrowding on the global scale. We'd need to take a lot of complex facts and findings on board, and even then it would be hard to settle things. But I want instead to focus on what might seem to be both an easier and a prior question – assuming there's space and resources are available, and that other practical problems can be set aside, just how many people ought there to be?

Let's make one further assumption. Let's just grant that there's something good about having some human beings in existence, and that it would be a bad thing if our species were to become altogether extinct. Still, we might continue with just a couple of people – a version of Adam and Eve – or with big numbers as today, or with billions, trillions, zillions more. What would be best? In particular, and setting aside the possible benefits and drawbacks to existing people, would it be better if there were even more people alive than in fact there are? There could be more. We could, together, make more babies. We could try to form colonies on the moon, or on Mars, and fill them with people. And suppose there's a God. He could, having created the one world, and seen that it's good, gone on to create millions more, throughout the universe, filling them all with plants, animals and human beings. So suppose we're given a godlike power:

> *Decisions*. It's the future. Even so, life on Earth is good. It's good, as well, on Mars, especially since they fixed the atmosphere and brought the temperature up to Californian standards. It took a long time, though, to get Mars sorted, a fit place for human habitation, and a long time to ship people the 50 million miles from planet to planet. It's easier now, with reproduction technology. All that's needed, thanks to the scientists' hard work, is that someone hits a button. And it's down to Max. It's all explained to him. Hit the right button, and nothing happens. Hit the left, and in a distant galaxy, near a distant star, there'll be a new planet formed, the planet Zog, with billions of people living good lives upon it. He's told he has to hit one button. But which one? One important detail – whatever he does, it will be neither good nor bad for people alive now. Max is left to decide.

That's to put the question on the large scale. And it's obviously, and may well always remain, science fiction. But, as I've suggested, the same question, though on a much smaller scale, affects many of us today, and affects us in practical terms. It's quite common for people to think about whether or not they want to start a family, and have children. Yet often too they think about whether this is something they ought to do. Life's good for the pair of them, and there's no strong urge to share it with anyone else. But then there's the thought, often encouraged by others, that they could have a child, or children, and give these new people the opportunity to sample the good things in life. Sometimes it's said that if you become a parent, your life will be much better than it is now. You'll benefit. But at other times the emphasis is just on the child. Suppose it's this. People say, have a child, give it a good life. Maybe you won't gain, but neither will you suffer. So think of others, of the child, and not just of yourselves.

Ought we, though, to be persuaded by this? It's different with adoption. There are children already in existence whose lives could be a lot better. Maybe some of us ought to adopt some of them. But there aren't babies, souls in limbo, waiting for bodies, and to be born. So if it's true that we ought to have children, supposing we can easily enough afford it, this isn't because it will be better for those children if we do. If we ought to have these children, it must somehow be better just in itself that there are more.

So large scale, a whole planet, and small scale, a single child, the question is in effect the same – ought there to be more people in existence, even when this isn't going to be better for those already living? Some people think all that matters is the quality of existing lives, and that unless they'll benefit, there's no reason at all to want new lives. Others think that, so long as the resources are available, whether it's within a family, a nation, the world population, or numbers through the universe as a whole, the more people there are, the better it is. And yet, even though this view is fairly widely held, both within philosophy and without, it's surprisingly difficult to find good arguments to support it. I'll mention here just two, neither of which really works. With the first it's easy to see, I think, where things go wrong, and why the argument fails. The second is a much better argument, and might seem to provide good reasons for thinking more is better. But in fact few people are really convinced by it, with most thinking there's a catch somewhere. Here's the first argument:

Saving and Starting. Consider just the worthwhile, or meaningful, or happy lives. Someone living such a life is drowning in a pool. It would be good to save this person's life, and if you could do this easily, you should. So, equally, it would be good to start such a life, and if you could do this easily, you should. If you and your friend can easily enough have a baby, then have one. And if you can easily enough create a new planet, then create.

Notice here that we're only thinking about good lives, lives that are worth living. And the suggestion is that if you could start such lives, at little or no cost, either to yourself or others, then you should do so. This isn't, though, merely to claim that it would be alright to start these lives. We can all agree with that. It's to claim, more strongly, that this is something you ought to do. But then the argument for this is poor. To save someone's life is to give them back the opportunity to continue with, and perhaps to complete the various plans and projects in which they were involved. You don't want to die, because you're only half-way through your book, or your garden, or your paragliding course. But while people can be harmed or frustrated or cut short by death, no one is harmed or frustrated or cut short by not being born in the first place. And so it's perfectly possible to agree that we ought to save existing lives, without agreeing that we ought therefore to start new lives as well.

So much, then, for the first argument. What about the second? It's easy enough to see how this argument goes, but harder, I think, to know just what to make of it:

> *Wretched and Joyous.* Contrast good and bad lives. Think about a life that is full of pain and agony from its first day to its last. And imagine there are no compensations, no possibility of appreciating music, or doing theoretical physics, or enjoying good jokes in spite of the pain. This life is wretched through and through. It would clearly be bad to live, and wrong knowingly to start, such a life as this. But then if it's wrong to start the wretched life, surely it's right to start the joyous life, the one we know will be full of pleasure and happiness from its first day to its last.

Forget all the objections about how we might learn from the wretched life, or about how these life and death decisions are not ours to make. We're thinking about the value of life just in itself, and not its side effects for other people. And we're thinking here not about ending a life, but rather choosing not to start it. It's hard to see what can be objectionable about that. And in the end almost everyone agrees that it would be wrong to start this wretched life, and for a couple to plan to have a baby if they knew it would live for just two or three weeks, always in extreme pain, and then die. But then if that's so clearly wrong, why isn't it equally clearly right to start a life when you know it will be well worth living?

Or more simply, if more wretched lives would be bad, then surely more joyous lives would be good? Yet even if it seems as if we should accept the apparent symmetry here, this argument is in practice unpersuasive, and the response of many philosophers is to try to discover where it goes wrong. It just does seem, that is, that the block on starting bad lives is much stronger and clearer than any mirror-imaged need to start good ones.

Let's leave this for now. Some of us – and when I talk to people about this, there seems to be a roughly fifty-fifty split – think that more lives would be better. But it isn't easy to find good reasons or arguments for this. I said at the outset, though, that I think there's a link between claims about numbers, and claims about quality. So we can focus on some questions about the quality of lives for a while, and come back to numbers later.

Good Starts

Lives can go better than they do. Which of us wouldn't want to be happier, healthier, with a better sense of humour, more intelligent, better looking? Most would. Those who don't usually have some special reasons – he's famous for looking just like this, the man she loves is already intimidated by how clever she is, and so on. Take account of the special reasons, and it becomes clear that, even here, we're looking for the better life.

And which of us wouldn't want our children to get off to a good start? The special reasons are even harder to apply here, and it would seem perverse or selfish not to care about the life they'll lead, and not to think that this life might be improved in fairly standard ways – health, intelligence, education, money, will all help. And so perhaps you should stop smoking, and cut down drinking while pregnant. Perhaps you and your partner should together read some books on child care, in preparation for the time ahead. And then, maybe, when that time comes, you should get them walking, talking, doing things as soon as you can, rather than sitting all day in front of the TV. You ought to watch their diet, think about schooling, consider buying them a pet, or making them a brother or sister. And so on.

It's important not to get carried away here. It would be strange to be utterly indifferent to your children's quality of life, but strange as well – whatever people might say – to do everything possible to give them the best start. After all, parents have got their own lives to lead. And if the next generation is important, so too is the generation alive now. Both matter. Still, even if you shouldn't do everything, you should surely do some things to increase their chances. There are some sacrifices we should make – let's not fuss about exactly how much – to improve the quality of future lives.

All this, I think, is fairly uncontroversial. But, as I said earlier, there are complications here, and this point might easily be confused with another, closely related but distinct nevertheless. This further point is controversial. And the confusion comes about because of matters concerning identity.

Different People

Here's an interesting fact. If Hitler hadn't invaded Poland, that fated September in 1939, almost none of us would be here today. For just think about it. That's well over sixty years ago. Not only were most of us not then born, but in the majority of cases our parents, and sometimes even our grandparents, hadn't even met. And if it weren't for the war – conscription, blackouts, enforced or restricted travel, long nights in air raid shelters – few of those meetings would have taken place. But then if our parents hadn't met, we wouldn't have been born.

What sort of fact is this? I think it's just one of those things. For it just so happens, and of course is nowadays well known, that both the sperm and egg carry important genetic material that affects the identity of the person who is later born. Things might have been different. And we can imagine a situation where the man's contribution is minimal – sperm just acts as a catalyst, so that whatever the sperm, and whoever it's from, the woman's child is the same. If that were so, then you could have had a different father. But as a matter of fact it isn't so. And as a matter of fact, if it weren't for World War II, and its multiple effects on who met who, most of us would never have existed. Consider, for example:

> *Swaps.* It's just a week after the funeral, and Gene and his mother are looking at old photos of the football team. There's his father, between two taller men, on the back row. And the captain, in the centre, holding the ball. His mother seems wistful, distracted. She says, 'You never knew, we never told you, but I almost married him, instead of your father.' He looks, sees his hair, his muscles, his comic book jaw, and he thinks, maybe it would have been better for me, if she'd gone off with him.

Does Gene make a mistake? Yes. It seems that events happening after conception affect the quality of a given life. So whether or not a pregnant woman smokes can bear upon the life of a particular child. But many events happening prior to conception will affect not only the quality, but also the identity of the child to be born. And none more so than swapping one man for another. Depending on the strength of his mother's affections for this other man, Gene should count himself lucky to be alive at all.

Here's another case, different in one notable, but in the end unimportant respect:

> *Delays.* Gina's always had these irritating allergy problems — asthma, bad reactions to food, over-sensitive skin. For a long time it was looked on as just one of those things, but in recent years doctors have suggested it might be linked with the work her mother did when she was pregnant. They'd not been married long, money was short, and she had this job in a chemicals factory. They made paints, dyes, solvents, a lot of it from substances that have since been banned. She didn't stay. There was a shortage of teachers, and a publicity campaign, and really good grants. So she packed it in and went to college. And now Gina often thinks it would have been better for her if her parents had waited six months or so, maybe a year, before having a child.

Is this a mistake? It isn't as obvious as in Gene's case, but here too the options are fewer than they might seem. Gina could not have had a better start to life, missed out on the allergies, if her parents had delayed having a family. For it's not only the parents who determine the identity of children, it's the timing as well. Again, it's the details of biology that make this so. Take an embryo, freeze it, and perhaps a particular person can be born later than would normally be the case. But, as in Gina's case, take a different, and later, sperm and egg, even from the same parents, and, because the genetic material is different, a different child will be born. Unconvinced? Suppose she has a sister, Jane, who is a year younger. If her parents had delayed and reduced their family, having just the later child, they would have had Jane, and not Gina. Jane's existence, like yours and mine, doesn't hinge on the existence or non-existence of some older sister.

These cases, involving first different parents, second different times, are not controversial. A different person is born. Another case might be more controversial, and its bearing on identity less straightforward:

> *Earlier and Later.* Sinead and Siobhan are already pregnant. But there are complications. Unless they undergo treatment their children will be blind.

But there's a difference. Sinead's child will go blind in later life, probably when she's in her thirties. Siobhan's child will be blind from birth. But the treatment is complex and risky to both mother and child. It's their decision, but doctors advise against it. After all, even if blind, life is still well worth living.

It's much later, and Sinead's child – call her Agnes – is losing her sight. She thinks, if my mother had had the treatment, and it had been successful, I wouldn't now be going through this, wouldn't soon be blind. And this is true. Agnes – the very same person – could have had a life which didn't involve her going blind. But what about Siobhan's child? He's James. And he thinks, if my mother had had the treatment, I wouldn't have always been blind. Is this true? Could the very same person have been sighted from birth?

There isn't an easy answer to this question. If we think identity depends upon the continuity of the body, then indeed James would have existed either way, blind or sighted, depending on the operation. For, after the embryo is formed, the same body continues to exist, even if altered in some respects. But if we think identity depends on psychology then it's less clear. Blindness makes a big difference, and had he been sighted, almost all of James's experience, his beliefs, attitudes, interests, relationships would have been different throughout his life. In one sense he'd have been a different person. And so in one sense, if Siobhan had had the treatment, James would never have existed, and another child, perhaps called James, perhaps not, would have existed instead.

Two views, then, and I'm not sure there's a way to settle it. It depends in part on what we think is important to identity, and depends too on the old nature/nurture debate. I'm assuming that much of our thinking, and much of our character, depends on our experiences, and how we're brought up. So if, as a one-day-old baby, I'd been adopted by a Japanese family, given a lot of fish, and trained as a sumo wrestler I'd have been, at the least, very different from the person I am today. But perhaps genes do more work than often we realize. And investigations with identical twins, separate at birth, often suggest that much of our character and personality is resistant to the influence of experience and environment, remaining substantially the same whatever happens to us.

We don't need to settle it, however. I raise it as a way of contrasting with, and separating out the clear and uncontroversial cases. Alter the parents, or – by some margin – the time of conception, and there'll be both substantial physical and psychological differences. In such a case a different person is born. Alter the embryo in such a way that changes occur, or are prevented, in later life, and the same person is benefited or harmed. The intermediate case, where the same organism leads a completely different life throughout, can from now on be set aside.

Go back a bit. I said that there are some sacrifices we should make to improve the quality of future lives. I said this was uncontroversial. But then I added that puzzles about identity might lead us to confuse the uncontroversial claim with another. So just what are these two claims? The first is this: if there's a particular life, a particular person, and we can fairly easily improve that life, then we should. And for certain, it's better, other things equal, if particular lives go better. A more controversial claim is this: if we can fairly easily choose one very good life over another, somewhat less good, then we should. It is, I think, less certain that, when the lives are different, it's better if good, rather than less good lives are lived.

Better People

Here, then, is a good question: is it better if the better lives are lived? Again, different people have different views, but when I ask around, it seems that most people think it is better. But is that right? Consider this case, a version of a now famous example given by Derek Parfit:

> *The Young Girl.* She's not pregnant yet, but Sharon really wants a baby. And she won't take the pill, or use other contraceptives. It's driving her mother, her teachers, her doctor, crazy. And they all tell her she should wait, have sex for the fun of it if she insists, but make sure no child is born. For just think about what it's going to be like for a baby now, when there's so little money, she's still at school, and chances are she wouldn't even know who the father was. No one wants to suggest that her baby would have a bad life, but it would certainly be less good than it might be, and he or she would be disadvantaged relative to many other children. Much better, then, to wait until she's older, more settled, more mature. Leave it for, say, ten years. She'll be able then to give her baby a much better start.

Suppose the arguments work, and she's persuaded to wait. Does she make the right decision? It's tempting to think she does. If you can give your baby a better start, at little or no cost to you or anyone else, then, surely, you should do so. There is a cost in Sharon's case – she wants a child now, and will be frustrated, irritated, difficult to live with, if she has to wait. But that's not a massive cost, and we can imagine that she's persuaded that it's clearly compensated by the better life ahead.

Notice, though, that there's a degree of ambiguity here. She'll give her child, in waiting, a better start, and a better life, But it's going to be a different child. The chances are there'll be a different father involved. And even if not, the time lag is still enough to ensure that a child born then must be a different person from any child she could have now. Suppose, to make this clearer, she wants a girl. If she has one now she'll call it Crystal. But tastes change. And a later child, still a girl, will get the safer name Anne. So, whatever else we might say of it, waiting isn't going to benefit or be better for Crystal. For her, it's now or never. But will waiting be better for Anne? Suppose she's set on just the one child, so that if she has Crystal, Anne will never be born. But she waits, Anne is born, and has a very good life. Is this better for her, to her benefit? Certainly not in any ordinary sense. Ordinarily we say someone is better off when we compare two situations in which they find themselves, and rank one of them above the other. Anne exists and has a good life. Yet this isn't in any ordinary sense a benefit. For she doesn't first find herself not existing, with existing then being better for her.

Will waiting be better for anyone? Very probably it will. It's likely to be better for Sharon's parents, her teacher, perhaps even her doctor, if she waits. It's likely, too, to be better for society as a whole, with the later child having less need for support from social services and then in time, because of her education, paying more in taxes. And it may well be overall better for Sharon herself, in spite of her frustration now, if she puts off having this child for some years. And these various benefits to existing people may well provide excellent reasons for waiting, and having, instead of Crystal, the later child Anne.

Here's another reason. Suppose she's persuaded that any child she has now will have a very bad life, a life not worth living. Imagine that doctors identify some physical problem that might, in time, be cured. If, as I've suggested, it's clearly wrong to bring into existence someone destined to have a wretched life, then she has, in light of this information, a very good reason for waiting, and having the later child.

Imagine that waiting is better for no one. And wait or not, the child's life is worth living. It's just that the later life is better. Should she, in these circumstances, wait, and have the later child? Many people, and many philosophers, Parfit included, think it's clear that she should. So they think, not only is it better if particular lives are improved but also that it's better if we choose the better lives to be lived. And, importantly, they think this is better, even when it's not better for anyone.

Links

Here, finally, is the connection I promised at the outset between numbers and quality. We were looking for an argument to support the view, held by many people, that it's better if more people are born. A good argument is hard to find. But now this is surely right: if we think it's better if the better lives are lived, we should think, also, that it's better if more lives are lived. So if Sharon should wait, and give birth to Anne rather than Crystal, she should have Anne anyway, whether or not Crystal was part of the plan. If it's better to have a good child rather than one that's only reasonably good, it's better – and maybe more obviously better – to have the good child than no one at all.

It's easy enough to understand my suggestion here, but harder, usually, to accept it. Here's an obvious objection. It's one thing to suggest that Sharon should wait, when she's already set on a child, but quite another to persuade her to have a child when, earlier or later, becoming a mother is no part of her plan. That's obviously way too much to ask. Well, often of course it is, but my suggestion isn't quite this straightforward. The point is that in persuading her to wait we're wanting her to make some sacrifice – for after all she's hoping for a child now – in order to bring about a better result overall. And my suggestion is only that, if this is right, she should make a similar sacrifice to bring about a good result overall. And it will be a good result. If it's better to have Anne rather than Crystal, even though it's better for no one, then it's better to have Anne rather than no child at all.

A second objection follows on from this. Maybe it's better to have Anne than Crystal, given she's set on a child, only because this is the least bad option. Better still, perhaps, to have no child at all. So if she isn't even thinking about a child then there's just no reason to encourage her to have one. But this misses an important point. We said all along that both Crystal and Anne would have lives worth living. And no one is suggesting the costs to society are so great that it would be better if these worthwhile lives never came into being. The only objection to Crystal is that Sharon could do better. And there's no objection to Anne at all.

And here's a third objection. Certainly we can rank and compare two lives, saying that one is better than the other, because, say, it's longer, or happier, or more meaningful. But it's far from obvious we can compare one life with no life at all. Comparisons depend on there being things in common in order to get off the ground. So it just doesn't follow, from Anne's having a better life than Crystal, that her life is better than nothing at all. Now there's something in this objection. But again it misses the point. For it's claimed that not only is Anne's life better than Crystal's, but its being better gives us a reason to prefer it. That's a further move. And my suggestion is only that if we have a reason to prefer the better life, then we have a reason to prefer this life to nothing at all. If it's better that better lives are lived – even though better for no one – then it's good that good lives are lived, even when good for no one.

Sharon's case is very like any number of real cases. And it's complicated, inviting thoughts about various practical concerns, in the way that real cases often do. It might be easier, then, to see the underlying point by thinking about a simpler, and more artificial case. So go back to the planets. And alter the situation a little. Max trapped his left hand in the spaceship door a week ago, and it still hurts. Other things equal, he'd prefer to use the right. But he's persuaded to use his injured hand, hit the left-hand button, rather than the right, in order to bring into existence Zog, where people have very good lives, rather than Zander, where their lives are moderately good. And my claim is that if he's going to make the sacrifice, hurt his hand, in this case, he should make the same sacrifice, hurt his hand equally, when, as in the initial situation, the choice is between Zog and no planet at all. If it's better to have a good planet rather than one that's only reasonably good, it's better – and maybe more obviously better – to have the good planet than nothing at all.

Better Lives?

Should there be more people? Yes, if there should be better people. If we ought to start the better of two lives, or the better of two planets, then we ought to start these lives, these planets anyway. That's my suggestion. But is it really true that we should start the better lives? Is it really better if these are the lives that are lived?

> *Tests.* She's retired now, after working most of her life in the supermarket. She's never thought of it as a bad life – she has friends, a nice home, never been really ill, touch wood – but it's often seemed it could have been better, and would have been better, perhaps, if she'd had a different job.

But she got off to a poor start at school, couldn't then get a lot of support from her mother, and so never really caught up. Sometimes it seems her uncle, always sticking his nose in, might have been right. It might have been better if she'd never been born, and her mother had waited, and had a different child, later, instead.

Rather than looking forward, we're now looking back on much of Crystal's life. Of course, she might never have such thoughts. And it might be wrong to encourage them. But suppose she does have them. Is she right to think it would have been better if the better life had been started, and that she'd never existed? Or think of a similar situation, concerning not which lives are best started, but which are best saved:

Sharks. There's a hurricane and their boat goes down, miles from civilization. They swim towards the desert island, but a shark attacks Alex, eats his legs, and Rob arrives there alone. He's glad to be alive, for even though there's virtually no hope of rescue there are fish, and papayas, and places to shelter. And he doesn't mind solitude. But he can't help thinking that it would have been better if he'd been killed, and Alex had survived. Alex had always fantasised about the island life – coming to know himself, writing his memoirs on palm fronds, watching the sun go down. Rob's life here will be good, but Alex's would have been better.

Here it's down to chance, or down to sharks, who lives and who dies. But still we might have thoughts about what would be best, and might agree or disagree with Rob's view that he should have died. And now contrast this with a further case, similar to this in that it's about saving lives, but different in that decisions need to be made:

Drugs. They promised not to target the hospital. But it was hit anyway, near the stores, and now blood, medicines, even bandages are in short supply. And, especially with the typhoid, there are lives to save. It's impossible to help everyone, and decisions need to be made. They can't afford to use drugs on the hopeless and near hopeless cases. They give priority to those with the greater responsibilities, those who are most needed – mothers with young children, the men from the peace commission, those among the injured who themselves have medical skills. And then, having done their best here, they try to save those who will have the longer or happier lives.

Doctors are always having to make such decisions, as there are always some limits on resources. And their decisions are often ones we can understand and agree with. Often, in saving younger lives, they're think-ing about those who can offer most to society, or about the better chances of recovery, or about family breadwinners. The doctors here do think about such things. And they put these people first. But then they focus on those promising longer and happier lives, believing this will be better overall, even if it doesn't bring about better consequences elsewhere. Are they right to do this?

I think all these people make a mistake. It's one thing to set a first life against a second, and then to claim that one of them is, overall, the better life. In all the above cases such judgements can, correctly, be made. But it's another thing to insist that it's better if the better lives are lived. Who is it better for? It's better, in these cases, for no one. So why is it better? It is, I think, impossible to say.

There is an objection here. It's been touched on, and set aside earlier, but it needs a further airing. Someone might say, it's better for Crystal if she's born and, similarly, better for Anne if she's born. So far it's a stand-off, but of course we should add that as Anne lives the better life, being born is, arguably, even better for her than it is for Crystal. And so it's best if her life is started. Yet this doesn't seem to me to be convincing. Each of them has just the one shot at life, and for each of them, life will be well worth living. And if the mother wants a child now that seems to me enough reason for Crystal, rather than Anne, to be born. Or take the hospital case. Though you and your friend both have good lives, you're a gloomy sort, while she's always full of beans. You both need treatment, but there's enough only for one. To me it doesn't seem fair that she should get it, just because she'll be a bit happier than you. To me it seems fairer that someone toss a coin.

Should There Be More, and Better, People?

I mentioned Hitler a while back. He, of course, was someone keen on the idea of there being, as he saw it, better people in existence. Most of us oppose almost everything he stood for. And so we reject any such blanket idea that Aryans are good and Jews are bad. We think it wrong to segregate, forcibly sterilize, eliminate people and groups of people. And those with handicaps and disabilities, physical or mental should, we believe, be helped rather than cast aside. The legacy of such opposition is still with us. Keith Joseph scuppered his chances of being Tory leader with a 1974 speech suggesting efforts be made to reduce the number of teenage pregnancies. Hans Eysenck, Arthur Jensen, and more recently the authors of *The Bell Curve*, have all been vilified for their allegedly scientific attempts to link, first, race and class with intelligence, and then intelligence, or its relative absence, with criminal and anti-social behaviour. Many of us detect, behind all such thinking, undeniable residues of the Nazi programme.

Take a broader view, though, and our attitudes to eugenics, to 'the science of good generation' are less clear-cut. Particularly in the first decades of the twentieth century, such ideas were more or less mainstream, with H.G. Wells and George Bernard Shaw only the best known of their advocates, and Bertrand Russell as at least a fellow traveller. And while we might today oppose both Hitler's methods and many of his more sweeping claims, the underlying notion, that given certain diseases and disabilities life is worse than otherwise it would be, is one with which we almost all agree. Many of us agree, too, that, provided the means are legitimate, it would be good both if these diseases and disabilities could be eliminated, and if steps could be taken to improve the quality of new lives. So abortion on quality of life grounds, designer babies, the aims of the human genome project, even while controversial, are all acceptable topics of conversation. While the emphasis here is often on individual cases and individual choice, there are issues too about larger and more public themes. So in Britain there are worries that the middle classes in particular aren't having enough children, while in the USA the corresponding concern centres on the differences in birth rates between, as the census forms have it, Caucasians and Hispanics. The language may be different, with eugenics as such rarely mentioned, but the concerns are the same.

Those opposed to such trends often go on about rights, the rights of the unborn, or the untrammelled right to reproduce. Or they deny that there are such things as handicaps and disabilities anyway. I'm suggesting a different tack. Even if we should hope to reduce, by appropriate means, the number of bad lives, those not worth living, it isn't at all clear that we should hope, as well, to swap reasonably good lives for those that are even better. And, of course, many diseases and handicaps, even if they lower the quality of life, still leave it as well worth living. So even if it wouldn't be a bad thing if only very good lives were lived, it wouldn't, so far as I can tell, be an especially good thing either.

And similarly for more lives. I've argued there's a connection here. If it would be better if the better lives were lived, then it would, as well, be better if more lives were lived. Catholics, in particular, have thought that, at least if other things are equal, we should go forth, multiply, and increase the number of lives. That, they've said, would be a good thing. And even those who don't expressly buy in to the Catholic view often think it would be better if there were more people in the world or, as the world seems now seems to be pretty full, on other planets. But again, it seems to me that even though it wouldn't be a bad thing if there were more people, it wouldn't be a particularly good thing either.

What does matter, it seems to me, is that actual lives are worth living. It matters as well that these actual lives are, where possible, further improved, so that they are even better than otherwise they would be. There are, as I say, limits to the sacrifices we should make here, but it's not unreasonable to ask us sometimes to help each other. Yet that's about as far as sacrifices need go. I wouldn't raise a finger either to bring a new world into existence, or to reject Zander in favour of Zog.

Chapter Ten

Does Reality Matter?

. . . by reality I mean shops like Selfridges, and motor buses, and the Daily
Express.

(T.E. Lawrence, 1929)

I hated that film *Shakespeare in Love*. If it had been just a story, made
up from start to finish, it wouldn't have been at all interesting. What was
supposed to make it interesting was that it was about Shakespeare. But
then it wasn't really about Shakespeare at all. He wasn't like that, didn't
say those words, did hardly any of those things. It claimed to be about
reality, but it wasn't. I didn't really like *The Matrix* either. It's a different
kind of film. Though clearly fiction from start to finish, it sets out to ask
a string of questions about the nature and importance of reality. Some of
these are good questions, but they tend to get lost in the fight between
good and evil, and the special effects. And it's too long.

Reality does matter to us. When we watch films about Shakespeare, or
Oscar Wilde, or Sylvia Plath, most of us do care that the details are more
or less accurate. We look to the film to tell us something of the truth
about what those people were like. Other films, like *The Matrix*, *1984*, or
The Truman Show, themselves reveal the extent to which people care
about reality, and how it matters that they are not swept along on a tide
of illusion, no matter how comforting that might be.

Some of these concerns with reality are more or less straightforward,
and easy enough to explain. One obvious and uncomplicated reason for
getting the facts right, seeing things as they are, is that it's often better
and easier for us if we do. To know how things are is to know something
of how they will be, and so to be better prepared for what happens next.
And often, the message in films and literature is that getting in touch with
reality makes for a richer, a happier, a more fulfilling life. But there are
some situations in which the concern with reality is harder to understand.
Someone wants to know the truth about their genetic make-up even
though they'll be unable to prevent the disease occurring anyway. Another

person insists on all the details of how, in a car crash, their sister died. A third seems obsessed with whether some comment from an ex-boyfriend, years ago, was sincere or merely polite. Does any of this matter? Why care about reality when it makes no difference to anything, when there's nothing in it for you?

Yet at other times a concern with reality is set aside. People often want to escape it – maybe with drugs and alcohol, or a fantastic holiday somewhere hot, or by getting absorbed in reality TV. They'll bury their heads in the sand, perhaps when ill, or when bad things are happening at work, or in relationships. They might be curiously indifferent about whether things are as they seem, as with fake or real diamonds, an improbably firm jaw, the colour of someone's hair.

All in all, then, there's a lot here that isn't clear. Just when does reality matter to us? How much does it matter? And, here's the philosophical question, ought it to matter? I'm going to consider first a number of familiar areas where these questions about reality are raised. Some of them connect back with themes in earlier chapters, while others are new. And then I'll move on to a less familiar area, one that will take more time to get clear about, and one in which the puzzle about reality is put in a more general form. Think about all this, and maybe we can better understand when, how, and why reality matters.

God

Does it really matter whether or not God exists? Will it, in the end, make any difference to our lives? A lot of people have agonized over religion, and spent years trying to decide whether there really is a God, or whether he's something we've imagined or invented. But is it important to settle this? Or is fretting about religion just a waste of time?

Probably most people agree that God, if there is a God, works in mysterious ways. Even if things were different centuries ago, no longer is he going to make himself obvious to us, appearing from the clouds, or parting the seas, or sending someone to perform obvious miracles on his behalf. And even if he first created and still now sustains the world and its contents, many believers agree that its existence doesn't prove that God exists. And many of them also accept that what we find in the world doesn't point clearly to God – there would be churches, martyrs, good people either way. Nor, perhaps, do things point in the opposite direction. There are, of course, sceptics and atheists who think it's certain he doesn't exist, arguing from cosmology, or evolution, or the unending occurrence of both moral and natural evil that we must be on our own here. But others, while denying God, will allow that there is no proof of their position. For many on both sides, then, God's existence, or not, is a matter of faith with, in everyday terms, little or nothing hanging on the upshot. So it doesn't matter whether or not he's real.

There are, though, two things missing here. First, most people believe that God, if he exists, will make a big difference to what, if anything, happens in the world beyond. If he exists, the good will be rewarded, and perhaps the bad will be punished, while if he's no more than an illusion then nothing at will happen, either way. So if there is a God, if he's real, then there may well be important consequences for the future. Even so, the initial point remains: whether he exists or not, God isn't, it seems, making any discernible difference to the here and now.

Second, although God himself might make no difference, belief in him often does. Compare these two:

Jack and Jill. They go up the hill together to get some water. They've spent the day gardening, and need to make sure the seedlings have plenty to drink. It's been a lot of work, and they're both pretty tired. But Jack is feeling good about life, good about the garden, and confident that within a matter of weeks they'll have lettuce, beans, radishes, and more. There'll be food to spare, and they'll be able to give some to their friends and neighbours. Jill has her doubts. If slugs don't get everything, it'll be the neighbour's cat again. The others can get their own food. And, anyway, it's always more work than he says, and, anyway, she'd rather have pizza. And why do they have to go *up* the hill for water? That's really weird.

They clearly have different attitudes to life. And suppose, as might indeed be the case, that these differences in attitude connect with their different beliefs in God. He knows there's no proof, but Jack believes God is somehow looking after everything, and that ultimately all will be well. Jill thinks that really we're all alone here, our lives shapeless, and forever at the mercy of fickle fortune. And these different beliefs infect almost every aspect of their lives, colouring all their responses and making for real differences in their daily existence. Because they have different beliefs about whether life is meaningful, their lives really are meaningful to different degrees. And we might go further. Not only are they different, but in many ways Jack's is the better life. He's more resilient, happier, more fulfilled. His belief in God is good for him.

Does it matter, given all this, whether or not God exists? There are two views. Some people will think it doesn't matter at all. Belief matters. It's better, like Jack, to believe in God if that makes for a better life. And it just doesn't matter if this belief is based, at bottom, on an illusion, a failure to get to grips with what is in the end a godless universe. Others insist that truth matters. And if there is no God, then it's better to believe that, even if it makes, as with Jill, for a more difficult life.

So which is it? I've jumped in at the deep end here, and find it harder to get clear about this case than some of those that follow. But because God, and religion, play a large part in so many lives, it's maybe worth discussing this first. And I think I want to side with the first group above. So far as this life is concerned, it's hard to see it much matters whether there is a God or not.

Art and Nature

We often take pleasure in looking at things. But for most of the time we have certain beliefs about the things we're looking at. Does it matter whether those beliefs are true? Think about a pair of cases:

Fakery. Beth and Saul never agree about holidays. He likes the city, she likes the country. Afterwards they compare notes. This year he tells her of how, after hours spent in front of the Vermeers in Amsterdam, he discovered that one of them was a fake. There'd been a threat from terrorists, so they'd taken down the real thing and put in its place a near perfect copy. And they'd told no one! She'd had a similar time of it. Up in the Lake District, she'd visited Tarn Howes on the advice of friends who'd been there the year before. After the best part of the day swooning over the beauties of nature she'd returned to her hotel, only to learn from some American with a guide book that the entire place was a Victorian fantasy – Disneyland before its time.

Both Beth and Saul are disappointed to discover that things were not as they seemed. But does it really matter? After all, it was the appearance – the lie of the paint, the trees against the lake – that attracted them in the first place, and these are just the same, whatever the reality behind them. Surely it's the appearance that matters?

People often think this, but it seems to me not quite right. Saul was looking forward to seeing a Vermeer, a particular painting by a particular artist, not just some pretty coloured surface. And Beth thought she was admiring a natural landscape – something that contrasts with human ingenuity. She too was interested in things beyond or deeper than mere appearance. Even so, even if we agree that they both cared about what they were seeing, I think we shouldn't agree that Beth and Saul are equally short-changed by how things turned out. Consider Saul's complaint that he was looking at a fake. This isn't quite right, if a fake is something made with the intention to deceive. For let's assume the copyist was simply trying to replicate the Vermeer as closely as possible. Sure, the museum authorities then used this copy to deceive the public, and perhaps more importantly, the terrorists, but we can well understand why. And then what seems to be important here is that the thing that Saul saw looked just like the Vermeer. And what he understood about the painting, and learned about art – how Vermeer used tiny specks of white to bring light into his pictures, how his interiors differed from those of his contemporaries, how it's hard to say for certain whether a camera obscura was used – was none of it all different, via this copy, than it would have been through the real thing. Contrast this with Beth. In her case, there's no attempt at fakery or deception at all. And she could easily have read a guide book herself. But she didn't, and was altogether confused by what she saw, thinking that nature could fashion a lake with just those contours, bring this variety of trees together, keep barren this craggy outcrop. Until she stands corrected, Beth has completely the wrong idea about what nature can do.

Beth and Saul both have a false belief about what it is they're looking at. But for Saul, this is, in effect, the only false belief he has. Beth, in contrast, gets many things wrong. And the experience that Saul gets, from looking at the copy, is exactly the experience he'd have had, were the original still in place. But the experience Beth gets from what is in effect a Victorian park is quite different from any experience she'd have had from the unmanipulated natural world. In her case, a connoisseur or expert wouldn't have been taken in, while in Saul's case he might well have been.

Here's a suggestion then. We often want to be in touch with reality, and for things to be as they seem. But when our experience is going to be the same either way, being in touch with reality doesn't really matter.

Betrayal

People often cheat on those that they claim to love. It can cause a lot of grief. But what if it doesn't?

> *Devious*. Jacques leads a double life. When he's in London he's the loving husband, the devoted father, the truly settled family man. When Alex, at work, got involved with a PA from a client company he was one of the first to mutter about the idiocy of it, the anguish he'd caused his wife, the complete disruption for the kids. And for what? But it's surely all bluff. For when he's in Paris – and that's pretty often – he spends a lot of his time with Nadine, meeting her in restaurants, galleries, the theatre. It's been over three years, now, this betrayal. And still Claire suspects nothing.

How does he get away with it? Well, it's common knowledge that he sees Nadine – she's pretty high up in the Paris office, after all, and there's no objection to their meeting, for business or for innocuous pleasure, from time to time. But no one knows just how much time they share, or how much of it is indoors, and at night. And he thinks, so long as he keeps it this way, so long as no one finds out, then there's no harm done.

Is he right about this? Is it true, as they often say, that what you don't know about can't hurt you? Or even if she remains in seemingly blissful ignorance, is he wronging, or harming Claire nevertheless? Think about how, if he's pressed, Jacques will try to justify or excuse what he's doing here. He's going to insist that his behaviour is making absolutely no difference to Claire, or to her life. Not only is she unaware of what he's up to, and thus not upset or distressed or hurt by his torrid affair, but their relationship is in no discernible way changed. He still buys her flowers, surprises her with romantic weekends in the Cotswolds, makes love in that French way. He still loves her, after all, even if no longer to the exclusion of all others. Contrast this situation with so many others, where as a result of an affair things turn sour within a marriage even though the betrayed person has no idea why. Nothing like that here. And so, because Claire's life isn't in any way worse than it was, it's hard to believe that anything bad is happening to her, and so hard to believe that Jacques has anything to feel guilty about.

In effect, Jacques is appealing here to the point made at the end of the previous section. In reality, he's having an affair. But Claire's experience is going to be exactly the same, whether he has the affair or not. For her, then, this reality doesn't matter. Or so he argues. And yet it's likely that only a handful of people, and perhaps a handful already involved in some similar adventure, will be altogether confident in that verdict. For the rest of us there'll be a niggling doubt. So let's explore this.

Imagine two futures for Jacques and Claire. In the first he does, three years later, make a slip. His credit card bills are suspiciously large, and Claire discovers them. Or he forgets to close down his laptop after some frantic bout of cross-Channel emails. Claire is devastated, her world collapses. No one will doubt that after this discovery things are bad for Claire. In the second future Claire dies, in a car crash, two years later. She never finds out about Nadine, and her entire experience, throughout her life, is exactly as it would have been had the affair never happened.

You might think that so long as there's some chance that Claire will find out, Jacques is behaving badly. No matter what Nadine means to him, it's bad to risk so much. But now if Claire dies, ignorant to the end, then relief – a lot was risked, but as it happens, he got away with it. And because he got away with it, nothing bad happened. Is this right? Suppose she does find out. I'd say that this discovery certainly makes her life worse, at least for a time. But when did the bad times begin? If there's nothing at all bad about undiscovered betrayal, then there can be nothing bad about the discovery of such betrayal. And so for Claire to be upset about this is utterly irrational. Few of us will agree. We think she's right to be upset just because she has for all this time been betrayed. Things have been bad for six years, even though she's only just discovered it. And if this is right, then things are bad for her, even if, because she dies, she never discovers it. And if that's right, then it's not true that all that matters is experience. Reality matters as well.

Again, there's room here to say something about belief. Claire thinks that Jacques is faithful to her, when in fact he's not. But of course most of us have false beliefs about a whole range of things, every day of our lives. We don't normally think that it's bad for us not to be in complete touch with the truth. Rather, it's bad when, based on some false belief, we come to a decision that turns out to make our lives worse. But this isn't happening to Claire. And a further point. There are two ways in which we might replace false beliefs with true ones. We can change reality. Or we can change the belief. It might seem clear that it would be better for Claire were Jacques to have been faithful throughout. But would it better for her, also, to learn the truth about his philandering? That, I think, isn't so clear.

Virtual Reality

It was more than thirty years ago that the American philosopher, Robert Nozick, devised one of the most famous thought-experiments in the history of philosophy. It goes a lot like this:

> *The Experience Machine*. We all know that life can be hard. And we'd like it to be better. Can scientists help? They say they can. And they invent a machine that promises much. You want to meet exciting beautiful people on a beach in Madagascar, drive a Ferrari in the Monte Carlo Grand Prix, climb Everest and drink champagne? They can arrange it. Decide just what you want to happen for, say, the next two years, let the scientists know, enter the machine, and those things will happen.
>
> Only they won't really happen. What the machine can offer is a virtual reality, a simulation, in every last detail, of the life you want to lead. You'll actually spend two years floating in a tank, kept alive with wires and tubes. But it will seem to you exactly as if there's sand, crowds, mountains, just as you'd planned. Reality will be one way, your experience another.

Imagine the technology here is perfect. Nothing will go wrong. As soon as you enter the machine, you'll have the experiences you've pre-selected, and with absolutely no suspicion that it's nothing more than a kind of dream. Of course, when you leave the machine, you'll realize that none of the seeming things really happened, but that should, or so the scientists say, strike you as a small price to pay for two years of thrills. And you can always enter the machine again, newly programmed, for a further two years.

Would you take up the scientists' offer? Would you swap two years of reality, with all its ups and downs, for two years of hand-picked experiences? Or would you stay put?

Nozick is confident that none of us, if we thought things through, would enter the machine. We might at first be tempted, for we might suppose that all that really matters is how our lives feel, from the inside, and we'll know that, once in the machine, all these feelings will be good. But give it more thought, and you'll come to see that reality, and being in touch with it, counts for a lot. And, on Nozick's account, machine life is close to death. Anyone spending a long time in such an environment would, he says, be a mere blob, with no hope of being a person of any particular kind, no ability to do anything, or make any difference to the world, and no chance of encountering any deeper or more meaningful existence than one a mere machine has on offer. But, he insists, these are all things we care about.

It can look like an open and shut case, then. Think about the experience machine, and you'll see that there's no substitute for reality. There's a world out there, and what we want is to rub shoulders with it.

Some details

Yet I'm not convinced. Think through the details of Nozick's thought-experiment, take special note of the various steps within it, compare some of the reactions that other philosophers have given, and it seems to me that a number of objections might reasonably be made.

First, there's a point about time. I'm suggesting here two years, with an option to renew. And, because coming out of the machine might give you such a low, this option could be one that you'd want to take up. But it's still your choice. You might be there for two years or you might, in the end, be there forever. Must it be at least two years? I don't think so, but Nozick's idea seems to be that none of us would want to spend a long time in the machine. Maybe it's OK for a wet afternoon, but not for six months.

Second, there are possible confusions about experience itself. Someone might think that the machine offers only certain pleasant sensations – the kind of warm glow that you might get when things go well. But this doesn't seem at all Nozick's idea. The machine offers us particular experiences, in full detail, and not just their generalized after-effects. A related concern is about the connection between experience and the thing experienced: someone might insist that you can only experience climbing Everest if you actually work your way up that particular mountain. But Nozick's idea is that you might at least seem to climb Everest, and so have at least the experience *as of* the real thing. So programme the machine, step inside, and it seems to you that you are actually there in Copacabana, drinking *mojitos*, feeling the sun on your back. And then, as in reality, it seems that you feel warm and drunk. So the machine gives you neither reality nor merely its broad effects, but a seeming reality along with its consequences.

Third, and related, there are points to be made about pleasure and happiness. Again, this is something we've touched on earlier. Some people insist that there's more to happiness than feeling, and that to be genuinely happy there needs to be some kind of match between inner states, and outer reality. So even if it's possible to have a pleasant life in the machine, you couldn't really be happy there. Even so, it could seem to you that you were happy. And you might, if tempted by the machine, think the difference between seeming happiness and real happiness just isn't important.

Fourth, Nozick insists that no one would get into the machine. But even if he means this, I suspect he means, as well, that no one should get into the machine. His idea seems to be that if we thought about it properly we'd realize that the price of entering is just too great. So anyone who did get in would be making some sort of mistake.

Our various desires

Someone tempted by the machine is supposed to think, according to Nozick, that all that matters is the flow of experience, and how things seem to us. A concern for any underlying reality strikes such a person as a mistake. But then, when at last the machine looms large before him, this person thinks again, finds he wants to be a certain way, do certain things, venture beyond the contrivance of an invented world, and he declines to enter.

Is this right? A number of people have thought it's obviously right, and we don't need Nozick's example to persuade us that more matters to us than mere experience. And even to sketch the kinds of things that any of us might well be concerned about is enough to show this.

Take my own situation. There are things I want for myself — to cycle the length of Italy, to get to the jazz club on Friday — things for other people — my girlfriend's headaches to disappear, my brother to pass his law exams — and things for the world — boring and humdrum, but I want both Venice and tigers to be saved. Think first about those cases involving other people. I know them both, and I want their lives to go well. There's nothing remotely puzzling about this, and nothing puzzling, either, about the insistence that I want more, here, than can be provided by the experience machine. I want reality to be a certain way, rather than merely for it to seem to be that way. Let's make this clearer:

> *A Helping Hand.* Your mother is on her own now. And she looks forward to your weekly visits for both physical and psychological support — someone to do the heavy work in the garden, help her with the crossword and the sherry, reminisce about years ago. Heaven only knows how long she'd survive without you. But then the scientists call. They offer two years in the machine, at a discount rate. And they promise it will seem to you that the visits continue, and that your mother is just fine.

Of course you won't accept. Anything might happen, and probably will, while you're in there. Especially if our activities are needed for the well-being of those we care about, we are unlikely to contemplate retreat into the machine.

And think about the more distant cases. I'm not going to save Venice, or tigers. To be honest, I'm not even going to do much to help. It won't matter to them how I spend the next two years. But still, I want reality to be a certain way, rather than merely for it to seem to me to be that way. I want Venice to be saved. The scientists assure me that for two years it will seem to me that the flooding is controlled, the buildings repaired but not over-restored, the cruise ships kept at a safe distance. But I want these things to be true, and not merely to believe they are true.

Finally, my own case. This jazz. It doesn't really matter that I get there – the radio or a CD is about as good. And what the machine offers would be exactly as good – it would give me precisely the sights and sounds of being at the concert itself. So why bother to go? Why bother with airports, cellophane and jet lag if it can seem that you're even now on the beach in Malaya? Why queue at Disneyland if a virtual reality helmet can give you the Space Mountain experience? And, love or sex, why care whether or not the other person is real? But for me too the experience machine has its limitations. I don't want merely to seem to do all that cycling, programming the machine and pedalling away. That would surely be cheating. Part of what I want is to find out if I could actually do it, with those mountains, that heat, and the various distractions. I want to see what kind of cyclist I am, rather than just pretend. And for that I need, not a period lying in some machine, but a bike, and Italy.

So there are many things that I'm interested in, and concerned about, that go way beyond the level of mere experience. And I'm nothing special – it's the same, more or less, for all of us.

Does this mean, then, that we'd be crazy, sacrificing way too much, were we to take up Nozick's offer? I don't think so. It's one thing to agree that more than experience matters, and another never to swap real life for a machine substitute. And there are three reasons why such a swap might be considered.

First, we might be persuaded that our concerns for reality will be satisfied anyway, even if we're in the machine. It matters that your mother gets her weekly visit. But suppose she is visited by someone who seems to her to be you, while you, in the machine, seem to visit her. Isn't that just as good, for both of you, as a more conventional visit? And they're so keen to get volunteers for the machine experiment that they promise me the best treatment for my girlfriend's headaches, and private coaching for my brother's exams.

Second, these concerns may not be able to be satisfied anyway. I want the tigers to be saved, but it's already too late. However much I care, there's no reason here for me to choose reality over experience. So rather than collect money and signatures, write to MPs, travel to India, I might as well take up the scientists' offer.

Third, we might think more carefully about what the experience machine can do for us, and try to make better use of it. So think again about your mother. You're reluctant to enter the machine, leaving her alone in the real world. And some other visitor might not be as good. But suppose she enters a machine as well, and gets there the experiences she wants, perhaps seeming to get even more and longer visits from you, perhaps seeming to be well enough to need these visits no longer. Wouldn't this be better for her, and make it easier for you to opt for machine life? And this is, of course, a general point. A lot of what we want to do in the real world is in effect remedial work. If we can use machines for a quicker fix, the need for those activities disappears. And think about my cycling. It's true that I don't want a merely ersatz ride, a poor copy of the real thing. But surely the experience machine offers more. I could programme it so that in every last detail it seems as if I'm cycling in Italy – I seem to get hot, tired, blistered, in the way of cars. And if part of the reason for going is to push myself, see if I can really do that distance, then again, within the experience machine it may well seem that I fail. It's a mistake to think that the machine can offer only pleasure and success; it offers the experiences we want, whatever they are. And so it's hard to see why Nozick thinks that anyone in the machine would be characterless, not a particular kind of person, a mere blob. I might, while there, discover that so far as cycling goes I'm determined or half-hearted, careful or reckless, a good map reader, or someone who's always getting lost.

In or out?

Our concerns with a reality beyond experience don't, then, straightfor-wardly rule out our using the experience machine. For it may be that those concerns are as well served, more or less, whether we're in or out. But now even if it isn't obvious that we should stay out, it doesn't follow that we should ever get in. Should we? Could there ever be a reason to prefer the experience machine to reality? It may well depend on what reality has to offer.

> *Brainwash.* Bud and Dean are living the good life. Every day now they're on the beach at Honolulu, sunbathing, learning to surf, eating pineapples, meeting girls. And fantastic shirts. Who would have thought, when they joined the marines, that they'd end up here?
>
> Except they're not really in Hawaii. And there are no girls. They're still in Korea, prisoners-of-war, stuck in a dark hole, deprived of sleep, on starvation rations of food and water. And there's no end in sight.

In reality, then, Bud and Dean's situation is far from good. Yet they're unaware of this, and believe instead that they're having a marvellous time. This is neither a matter of chance, nor anything they've chosen for themselves, but is, of course, part of the Koreans' plan – brainwash them, soften them up and they'll maybe reveal the next stage of the war plans. That would be a bad thing. Perhaps it's better to know you're being tortured, and remain loyal, than, seemingly in Hawaii, to betray your country. But suppose this isn't going to happen. They give nothing away. And compare their lot with the other prisoners, Ged and Matt. The Koreans try a different tack with them, and they're fully aware of the prison, the guards, and their daily encounters with the torture machines. Why think their situation, in touch with reality, is in any way better than that of Bud and Dean?

Some of the objections to the experience machine assume that reality is best, and that we'll prefer bitter truth to comfortable delusion. But surely it depends on how bad reality is. Take an even more extreme case. Life might be so wretched that you think you'd be better off dead. But if death can be better than the reality of your existence, surely a make-believe life can be better as well? So even if there's always something to be said for reality, it's not clear why it should always win the day.

But is there always something to be said? In Bud and Dean's case reality is bitter, the delusion certainly comforting. And when experience within the machine is vastly different from that without, it might seem that in some situations the former is to be preferred. But what about cases where the experiences are the same? You can climb Everest, and see the view, or you can seem to climb, and seem to see. And suppose there are no further differences to take into account. So it's not as if, for example, the machine is cheaper, or safer than reality. And it's not as if memories of the real thing are longer lasting, or more vivid. Now it might seem that when everything else is the same, reality has the edge. And of course when everything else is the same there's still one difference. When you're in the machine you believe, but falsely, that you're climbing Everest. When you're on the mountain your beliefs are true. That might be why reality has the edge. Think instead, though, about a bad situation. Think about Ged and Matt. Is it better actually to be in a hole, tortured, with no chance of escape, than merely to seem to be? You might think there's some value in being in touch with reality when that reality's good. But it seems odd to think there's the same value when reality is bad.

Where Are We Now?

In thinking about reality, and whether it matters, it's been assumed more or less throughout that we know what reality is, and that we're all, for most of the time, up against it. And so the question of whether reality matters is in part the question of whether all this – Coca-Cola, global warming, plasma TV, war on terrorism – matters. But what if we're wrong? I said there were some good questions in *The Matrix*. This, more or less, is a scene from the film:

> *Colour Coding.* There's nothing particularly special about you, or your life. You're a more or less typical product of early 21st-century society, with the usual string of irritations at work and with your family, the usual distractions and compensations – a couple of holidays a year, lots of DVDs, golf – and, as far as can be expected, a reasonably secure future. But then you're somehow persuaded that this is all an illusion and that absolutely nothing in the world is real. Except you. You're offered a choice of two pills. Or, as you now understand, two seeming pills. Take the red one and you'll discover what the underlying reality is. Take the blue one and your seeming life will continue just as it was before. And, of course, for it to continue just as before requires that you'll forget completely your discovery of the illusion, and the offer of the pills. So you will forget.

What this suggests, of course, is that for all you know you might be in an experience machine right now. And inside the machine this apparent offer is apparently made. You can stay inside, with the illusions to continue, or you can exit, and find out what reality has in store. And we can clarify a handful of details. First, you are certainly real. If you take the red pill you'll discover what reality is. And you'll remember the illusory world you've left behind. You'll be able to compare them, and think about the wisdom of your choice. I say that you're real, but though you have something like a human mind, you might not be a human being. Second, you don't know whether other people are real or not. Perhaps a few are, but perhaps they're all part of the illusion. To take the red pill might be to discover that you're all alone, or it might be to lift the veils of illusion from others as well. Third, there are no further pills. And your decision is irreversible.

Would you take this pill? Some people might. Life might be really bad for them, or they might have a strong taste for adventure, or they might believe that they've been in some sense chosen for this. But I wouldn't. If I'm in an experience machine now I'm happy to stay put.

Does Reality Matter?

It often matters that we know the truth about things. For often, if we do, things will go better for us. Even if it tastes good, it's better to know whether the food's been poisoned. But often too, it doesn't matter that we live very much in ignorance. I know almost nothing about Byzantium, and that doesn't matter. In some cases, however, there's a puzzle. These are ones in which although it might at first seem to us to matter that we know the truth, it's not easy to say why. Yet though they all raise some questions about reality, the cases discussed here are not all the same. They resemble, and contrast with one another in different respects. And we tend to react to them in different ways.

So where the existence of God is concerned, although what we believe about him matters, and makes a difference to our lives, the reality itself arguably doesn't. But while some people will think it's better to believe in God, if it makes life better, others will think it's better to know the truth, even if life then goes worse. And it's similar with Claire's betrayal. Whether Jacques is faithful or not, her experiences will be the same. But many people will think, first, that it's nevertheless bad that she's being betrayed and, second, that it would be better for her to know the truth.

The cases involving Beth and Saul are similar to one another, and to those above in one respect. They both feel disappointed that things were not as they seemed. But in other respects there are differences. Whether the painting is genuine or not, Saul's experience will be the same. And my suggestion is that in such a case, it doesn't matter that he sees the real thing. But in Beth's case real nature and simulated nature are going to offer different experiences. So what she sees does matter.

One puzzle here is why Saul's case is different from Claire's. For both of them, experience will go a certain way whether or not things are as they seem. But suppose they discover the truth. It's easy to sympathize with Claire, less easy, or so I've suggested, to sympathize with Saul. In his case alone I want to say that reality doesn't matter. But what's the difference? I haven't given a good explanation of this. And the reason is, I don't know.

All these cases, even that of God, are concerned with details, compared with the experience machine. For the suggestion there is that, for long periods at least, nothing may be as it seems. Would that be a bad thing? I think Nozick is right to suppose that we care about more than experience, but wrong to think that we've therefore got good reasons not to get into the experience machine. But of course, caring about more than experience already assumes that there is more than experience to care about. Perhaps there isn't. And perhaps Nozick's fiction might already be fact. But, I'm suggesting, not to worry.

Notes and Further Reading

1 Where Can I Find Answers?

p. 1 *Waiting for Godot*, along with other works relevant to the themes of this book, is in Samuel Beckett's *Complete Dramatic Works*.

p. 5 Most of what we know about Socrates – his philosophical concerns, his trial, his attitude to his impending death – comes from Plato's dialogues, especially the *Euthyphro*, the *Apology*, the *Crito* and the *Phaedo*. They're available in many modern editions.

p. 9 Those of Kant's views that I refer to here come from his short essay, 'What is Enlightenment?' This, along with other short and readable pieces, can be found in *Perpetual Peace and Other Essays*.

p. 12 I came across this story about Carneades in *The Civilization of Rome*, by Donald Dudley. But it is widely reported.

p. 12 Hume's scepticism is a theme in both his *A Treatise of Human Nature* and *An Enquiry Concerning Human Understanding*. Kant refers to Hume's rousing him from his 'dogmatic slumber' in his *Prolegomena to Any Future Metaphysics*.

p. 13 Schopenhauer in his gargantuan *The World as Will and Representation*, Nietzsche all over the place.

p. 13 Wittgenstein aims at system in his *Tractatus Logico-Philosophicus*, but then is, seemingly, anti-system in his *Philosophical Investigations*.

Further reading

Good introductions to philosophy include Simon Blackburn, *Think*, Nigel Warburton, *Philosophy: The Basics*, and, much shorter, Thomas Nagel, *What Does it All Mean?* Alain de Botton's *The Consolations of Philosophy* is good at arguing that dead white men shouldn't all be forgotten.

Two useful websites, both with a range of materials, including much that is relevant to this book, are: http://plato.stanford.edu/contents.html This is an excellent online encyclopaedia of philosophy. http://www.philosophytalk.org/

This is a radio programme, with previous material archived, and thus still available. It's well worth looking at, and listening to.

2 Is Life Sacred?

p. 16 Some of Mary Wollstonecraft's views about the value of animal life can be found in her *Original Stories from Real Life*.

p. 16 Nietzsche in Turin, recounted in Ronald Hayman's *Nietzsche: A Critical Life*.

p. 18 For these distinctions between different sorts of value, see Ronald Dworkin's, *Life's Dominion*.

p. 22 'A man is really ethical . . .' is from Albert Schweitzer's *Civilization and Ethics*.

p. 24 For a good discussion of some of the views here, see *Utilitarianism, For and Against*, by J.J.C. Smart and Bernard Williams.

p. 24 For a discussion of anencephaly and moral issues, see Peter Singer's *Rethinking Life and Death*.

p. 27 For a discussion of Chatterton's suicide, see Al Alvarez, *The Savage God.*

p. 28 David Hume's *Dialogues Concerning Natural Religion*, unpublished in his lifetime, is a masterpiece. There are many modern editions available.

Further reading

Ronald Dworkin's *Life's Dominion*, gives the best discussion of the sanctity of life, both readable and detailed, that I know of.

Much shorter discussions can be found in a number of books, including Peter Singer, *Practical Ethics*, the same writer's *Rethinking Life and Death*, Jonathan Glover, *Causing Death and Saving Lives*, and Rosalind Hursthouse, *Beginning Lives*.

Michael J. Coughlan, *The Vatican, the Law and the Human Embryo* offers a close account of the Catholic Church's position on issues concerning the sanctity of life.

3 Is It Bad to Die?

p. 32 Many of Epicurus' surviving writings can be found in *Hellenistic Writings: Introductory Readings*. Lucretius' ideas on death are found in his poem *De Rerum Natura*, with various editions and translations available.

p. 33 More on Democritus – introductory comments, fragments, accounts by contemporaries – can be found in Jonathan Barnes, *Early Greek Philosophy*.

p. 33 'Accustom thyself to believe . . .', Epicurus, *Letter to Menoeceus*.

p. 35 Several of Montaigne's essays deal with matters relating to this book. See the *Complete Essays*.

p. 35 Boswell's account of Hume's death appears in his private papers.

p. 35 'Death is not an event in life', Ludwig Wittgenstein, *Tractatus Logico-Philosophicus* 6.4311.

p. 35 '. . . specious stuff that says . . .', Philip Larkin, 'Aubade', in *Collected Poems*.

p. 38 Jean-Dominique Bauby, *The Diving Bell and the Butterfly*.

Further reading

The topics of this and the following chapter, including the deprivation view, are well discussed in a number of books, including Fred Feldman, *Confrontations with the Reaper*, F.M. Kamm, *Morality, Mortality*, and Jeff McMahan, *The Ethics of Killing*. Two very useful collections are John Fischer (ed.), *The Metaphysics of Death* and Peter French and Howard Wettstein (eds), *Life and Death: Metaphysics and Ethics*.

For literary and cultural approaches to death and dying, see especially, Philip Ariès, *The Hour of our Death*, Jonathan Dollimore, *Death, Desire and Loss in Western Culture* and, for a particular kind of death, Al Alvarez, *The Savage God: A Study of Suicide*.

4 Which Deaths Are Worse?

p. 46 For much more on psychological connectedness, see especially Part III of Parfit's *Reasons and Persons*.

p. 47 For more on the mental life of animals, see David de Grazia, *Taking Animals Seriously: Mental Life and Moral Status*.

p. 49 There's a 1982 biopic about Frances Farmer called, perhaps unsurprisingly, *Frances*.

p. 49 For important, though sometimes difficult, discussions of death at different ages see Jeff McMahan's *The Ethics of Killing*.

p. 52 'Tell them I've had a wonderful life', quoted in Ray Monk's biography, *Ludwig Wittgenstein: The Duty of Genius*.

p. 54 Questions about posthumous harms are explored in some detail in Joel Feinberg's *Harm to Others*.

p. 54 This story about Kafka is described in Max Brod's biography of the writer.

p. 56 Look up 'German cannibal' and 'Alder Hey Hospital' on the web for more on two of the controversial issues here. For the third, see: http://www.bodyworlds.com.sg/en/news-01.htm

5 Might I Live On?

p. 60 For more on demythologized religion, see the modern classic, *Honest to God*, by Bishop John Robinson, and *The Sea of Faith*, by Don Cupitt.

p. 62 'Behold, I show you a mystery . . .'. St. Paul, I Corinthians, 15, 51–5.

p. 63 For a fuller discussion of the cannibal story, see Linda Badham's 'Problems with accounts of life and death', in P. Badham and L. Badham, *Death and Immortality in the Religions of the World*. As the title suggests, there's much more here that's relevant to this chapter.

p. 66 Socrates' views about the afterlife are best seen in the *Phaedo*.

p. 67 See especially the *Meditations* (many editions) for Descartes' dualistic account.

p. 68 See H.D. Lewis, *The Self and Immortality*, for a vigorous defence of immortality understood along dualist lines

p. 70 For much fuller accounts of reincarnation beliefs see various entries in Mircea Eliade's *Encyclopedia of Religion*.

p. 73 My story, *The Power of Prayer*, is adapted from one by Hume, in his sceptical account of miracles, in his *An Enquiry Concerning Human Understanding*. This is a great book, and there are many editions available.

p. 75 For more accounts of so-called near-death experiences, see Mark Fox, *Religion, Spirituality and Near Death Experiences*.

p. 75 'A handsome man in a shining robe was my guide . . .', Bede, *The Ecclesiastical History of the English Nation*.

Further reading

For collections of views on life after death, see Stephen T. Davis (ed.), *Death and Afterlife*, and Paul Edwards (ed.), *Immortality*.

The website www.wabashcenter.wabash.edu/Internet/front/htm gives access to a wealth of information on both religion in general and philosophy of religion in particular, including, of course, the topics discussed here. It is, though, a huge site, and it can be difficult to find one's way around.

6 Should I Take the Elixir of Life?

p. 78 'The true servants of Allah . . .'. This is from the Koran, of course. But I found it in *The Oxford Book of Death*. There are hundreds of useful entries here, including the two below.

p. 78 'At ninety they lose their teeth and hair . . .' from Jonathan Swift's *Gulliver's Travels*.

p. 79 'To be thirty-five for two years . . .', from Michael Frayn, *Constructions*.

p. 81 'Life should not last so long!' from the libretto of *The Makropulos Case*. The original by Janáček, based on Čapek's play, this translation by Decca, the Mackerras performance, 1979.

p. 81 Williams' paper, 'The Makropulos case: reflections on the tedium of immortality' is in the Fischer collection referred to in Chapter 3. It's also in Williams' own collection, *Problems of the Self*, where there are also a number of papers relating to Chapter 7.

p. 81 Thomas Nagel is among those who think Williams has things wrong here. See his paper, 'Death' , either in the Fischer collection, or in his own *Mortal Questions*.

p. 85 'a boredom connected with the fact . . .', Williams, 'The Makropulos case'.

p. 90 Recent fictional accounts of the tedium of immortality include Julian Barnes' finely comic close to *A History of the World in 10½ Chapters*, and the much darker *The Body* by Hanif Kureishi.

7 Who's Who?

p. 93 The English philosopher John Locke put forward the mind view in the seventeenth century, suggesting that if the mind of a prince somehow entered the body of a cobbler, then that humble cobbler would be the prince. More recently, the mind view has been advanced by the American philosopher Sydney Shoemaker. See his *Self-Knowledge and Self-Identity*.

p. 94 Ovid's *Metamorphoses* has a wealth of fantastic transformation stories. Interestingly, in only a few cases are these seen as threatening identity. Ted Hughes has translated or versioned many of them, in *Tales from Ovid*.

p. 94 I say it's 'fairly clear' that with the Teletransporter a body disappears completely and then a new one is formed. But is that really right? Or do atoms, or particles move? It is, of course, possible to pursue this at length on aficionados' websites. See, for a start: http://www.startrek.com/startrek/view/library/technology/article/70285.html

p. 95 For more details on the Twinkie defence, and its elevation to urban myth, see http://www.danfingerman.com/dtm/archives/000073.html

p. 96 The body view, too, has well-known supporters, perhaps most notably Bernard Williams, who seems to emphasize the whole body, more or less, and Thomas Nagel, who focuses on the importance of the brain.

p. 97 My *Beyond Torture* and *Pain or Gain* (p. 98) stories are adapted from some of Williams' thought-experiments in 'The self and the future'. This, along with further essays on personal identity, is in his *Problems of the Self*.

p. 101 This ship problem – often specified as the ship of Theseus – is a perennial of philosophical discussions about identity.

p. 104 The closest continuer account is developed and put forward by Robert Nozick, in his mammoth *Philosophical Explanations*.

Many of the discussions and views in this chapter derive from my reading of Part III of Derek Parfit's *Reasons and Persons*. Indeed, almost everything written on this topic in the past 20 years takes, and has to take, Parfit into account. Were it not for his book, this book wouldn't have been written. Other books on the topic include Harold Noonan, *Personal Identity*, Peter Unger, *Identity, Consciousness and Value*, and collections edited by Amélie Oksenberg Rorty, *The Identities of Persons* and John Perry, *Personal Identity*.

On identity more generally see especially Saul Kripke's highly influential and highly readable *Naming and Necessity*. This is a modern classic.

8 Is It All Meaningless?

p. 111 'We begin in the madness of carnal desire . . .', Arthur Schopenhauer, *Essays and Aphorisms*. This collection includes many of Schopenhauer's more seductive writings on the meaning and value of life.

p. 119 For more on Larry Flynt see, for example, the 1996 film, *The People vs. Larry Flynt*.

p. 122 'Meaning arises when subjective attraction . . .' from an essay by Susan Wolf: 'Happiness and meaning: two aspects of the good life'.

p. 124 Nagel discusses this in 'The absurd' in his *Mortal Questions*. His central idea there, that of an irreconcilable clash of perspectives, is further developed in *The View from Nowhere*. The last chapter here is especially relevant to the ideas of life, death and meaning.

p. 125 Camus' *The Myth of Sisyphus* has motivated much of the more recent interest in the question of meaning, but Jean-Paul Sartre's *Nausea*, Samuel Beckett's plays, especially *Waiting for Godot*, *Happy Days*, and *Endgame*, are similarly influential existentialist, or quasi-existentialist, texts. Behind all these, for many people, stands Dostoevsky's *Notes from Underground*.

p. 125 'Ring down the curtain . . .', quoted in *The Oxford Book of Death*.

p. 127 See, for example, Chekhov's *Three Sisters*, and especially the exchange between Masha and Toozenbach in Act 2.

p. 127 '"I also know," said Candide', Voltaire, *Candide*.

A pair of books, Oswald Hanfling. *The Quest for Meaning*, and his edited collection, *Life and Meaning: A Reader*, together comprise a number of classic and contemporary writings on the topic (including Tolstoy, Schopenhauer and Nagel) and a commentary on them. More recent collections include E.D. Klemke (ed.),

The Meaning of Life and Joseph Runzo and Nancy Martin (eds), *The Meaning of Life in the World Religions*. John Cottingham's *On the Meaning of Life* is a short and stylish book which is more sympathetic to the role of religion in giving life meaning than I have been here. For a very useful summary of a range of views, see Thaddeus Metz, 'Recent work on the meaning of life'. And for a very recent work, look at Julian Baggini's *What's it all About? Philosophy and the Meaning of Life*.

Douglas Adams' *The Hitchhiker's Guide to the Galaxy* is famous for its numerical interpretation of life's meaning. But I've never read it. Aldous Huxley's *Brave New World* is a twentieth-century classic dealing with the threats to meaning from modernization and progress. I have read this one.

Finally, the website www.phil.onemonkey.org contains responses from a number of philosophers working in Britain to a questionnaire asking them about the meaning of life. It makes for interesting reading.

9 Should There Be More, and Better, People?

p. 131 Philosophers who think that, other things being equal, more is better include Jonathan Glover, John Leslie, and Stuart Rachels. The latter's 'Is it good to make happy people?' is full of interesting arguments, some of which figure in my chapter.

p. 133 For an emphasis on good starts, see Julian Savulescu, 'Why we should select the best children'.

p. 134 See here especially the opening to Part IV of *Reasons and Persons*.

p. 136 My 'Identity and disability' pushes the idea that given a significantly different environment, a different person will be born.

p. 137 This case of the young girl closely follows one given by Parfit, in *Reasons and Persons*.

p. 139 I've attempted this argument before, in 'More lives, better lives'.

p. 143 For more on all this, see works by Hans Eysenck (for example, his autobiography, *Rebel with a Cause*, or *Intelligence: The Battle for the Mind*), by Arthur Jensen (*Environment, Heredity and Intelligence*) and, perhaps most notoriously, Herrnstein and Murray (*The Bell Curve*).

p. 143 'The science of good generation' is offered as a definition of eugenics in *The American Journal of Eugenics* (1906). I came across it at www.emmerich1.com/EUGENICS.htm

p. 143 Shaw's play, *Man and Superman*, explores a number of ideas relating to future societies. See also some of the works by his near-contemporary, H.G. Wells, including *War and the Future* and *The Conquest of Time*.

Further reading

As with Chapter 7, much here derives from Derek Parfit's arguments – this time in Part IV – in *Reasons and Persons*. The whole of that part is a fascinating, even if sometimes convoluted, discussion of ideas related to the themes of this chapter.

Two collections that deal with issues concerning future generations are Ernest Partridge (ed.), *Responsibilities to Future Generations*, and Peter Laslett and James Fishkin (eds), *Justice Between Age Groups and Generations*.

Discussion of quality of life issues appear in many books dealing with medical ethics. See, for example, Jonathan Glover, *Causing Death and Saving Lives*, John Harris, *Wonderwoman and Superman*, and, though harder, several of the essays in John Broome, *Ethics out of Economics*.

10 Does Reality Matter?

p. 146 Does God exist? For arguments, for and against, see, for example, *The Miracle of Theism* John Mackie, *Is There a God?* Richard Swinburne, and *Atheism and Theism*, J.J.C. Smart and J.J. Haldane.

p. 149 Good discussions of the value of fakes, forgeries, copies in art and nature can be found in Robert Elliott, *Faking Nature* and Denis Dutton, *The Forger's Art: Forger and the Philosophy of Art*.

p. 150 The idea that even undiscovered betrayal is bad, and a harm for the person betrayed figures in Nagel's essay, 'Death', in *Mortal Questions*. The discussion there isn't long, but it has been most influential.

p. 152 The Experience Machine was invented by Robert Nozick in his controversial and provocative *Anarchy, State and Utopia*. It appears again, in slightly different form, in his later *The Examined Life*.

p. 152 'A mere blob' is Nozick's own phrase here.

p. 157 My story, *Brainwash*, derives from the 1962 film – a political thriller – *The Manchurian Candidate*.

Further reading

As I said, I'm not keen on *The Matrix*. But Malt Lawrence is. And in *Like a Splinter in Your Mind: the Philosophy behind the Matrix Trilogy* (Blackwell, 2004) he explores a whole bunch of good questions including, of course, many of those discussed here.

Select Bibliography

The works listed here include most of the books and articles referred to in the previous chapters and many of those first mentioned in the notes and further reading. But it excludes films, musical works, and websites. In many cases there are, or have been, different editions. I have not tried always to give either the first or the last, but one that has been widely available.

Adams, Douglas (1979) *The Hitchhiker's Guide to the Galaxy*. London: Pan Books.

Alvarez, Al (1974) *The Savage God: A Study of Suicide*. Harmondsworth: Penguin.

Ariès, Philip (1981) *The Hour of Our Death*, trans. H. Weaver. New York: Alfred A. Knopf.

Badham, P. and Badham, L. (1987) *Death and Immortality in the Religions of the World*. Oxford: Pergamon.

Baggini, Julian (2004) *What's it all About? Philosophy and the Meaning of Life*. Cambridge: Granta.

Barnes, Jonathan (1987) *Early Greek Philosophy*. Harmondsworth: Penguin.

Barnes, Julian (1990) *A History of the World in $10^{1}/_{2}$ Chapters*. London: Pan-Picador.

Bauby, Jean-Dominique (1997) *The Diving Bell and the Butterfly*. New York: Random House.

Beckett, Samuel (1990) *The Complete Dramatic Works*. London: Faber.

Bede (1935) *The Ecclesiastical History of the English Nation*. London: Dent.

Belshaw, Christopher (2000) 'Identity and disability', *Applied Philosophy* 17.

Belshaw, Christopher (2003) 'More lives, better lives', *Ethical Theory and Moral Practice* 6.

Blackburn, Simon (1999) *Think*. Oxford: Oxford University Press.

Boswell, James (1931) *Private Papers of James Boswell*, eds Geoffrey Scott and Frederick A. Pottle, vol. xii, New Haven, CT. Yale University Press.

Broome, John (1999) *Ethics out of Economics*. Cambridge: Cambridge University Press.

Camus, Albert (2000) *The Myth of Sisyphus*, trans. J. O'Brien. Harmondsworth: Penguin.

Cottingham, John (2003) *On the Meaning of Life*. London: Routledge.

Coughlan, Michael J. (1990) *The Vatican, the Law and the Human Embryo*. Iowa City: University of Iowa Press.

Cupitt, Don (1984) *The Sea of Faith*. London: BBC.

Davis, Stephen T. (ed.) (1989) *Death and Afterlife*. London: Macmillan.

De Botton, Alain (2000) *The Consolations of Philosophy*. London: Hamish Hamilton.

De Grazia, David (1998) *Taking Animals Seriously: Mental Life and Moral Status*. Cambridge: Cambridge University Press.

Descartes, René (1986) *Meditations on First Philosophy*, trans. John Cottingham. Cambridge: Cambridge University Press.

Dollimore, Jonathan (1998) *Death, Desire and Loss in Western Culture*. London: Routledge.

Dostoevsky, Fyodor (2000) *Notes from Underground*, trans. Michael R. Katz. New York: Norton.

Dutton, Denis (1983) *The Forger's Art: Forgery and the Philosophy of Art*. Berkeley, CA: The University of California Press.

Dworkin, Ronald (1993) *Life's Dominion: An Argument about Abortion and Euthanasia*. London: HarperCollins.

Edwards, Paul (ed.) (1992) *Immortality*. New York: Macmillan.

Eliade, Mircea (ed.) (1987) *The Encyclopedia of Religion*. London: Macmillan.

Elliott, Robert (1997) *Faking Nature*. London: Routledge.

Enright, D.J. (ed.) (1987) *The Oxford Book of Death*. Oxford: Oxford University Press.

Epicurus (1988) 'Letter to Menoeceus'. Many of Epicurus' surviving writings can be found in *Hellenistic Writings: Introductory Readings*, trans. Brad Inwood and L.P. Gerson. Indianapolis: Hackett.

Feinberg, Joel (1984) *Harm to Others*. Oxford: Oxford University Press.

Feldman, Fred (1992) *Confrontations with the Reaper*. Oxford: Oxford University Press.

Fischer, John Martin (ed.) (1993) *The Metaphysics of Death*. Stanford, CA: Stanford University Press.

French, Peter and Wettstein, Howard (eds) (2000) *Life and Death: Metaphysics and Ethics*. Oxford: Blackwell.

Glover, Jonathan (1977) *Causing Death and Saving Lives*. Harmondsworth: Penguin.

Hanfling, Oswald (1987a) *The Quest for Meaning*. Oxford: Blackwell.

Hanfling, Oswald (ed.) (1987b) *Life and Meaning: A Reader*. Oxford: Blackwell.

Harris, John (1992) *Wonderwoman and Superman*. Oxford: Oxford University Press.

Hayman, Ronald (1982) *Nietzsche: A Critical Life*. Harmondsworth: Penguin.

Hughes, Ted (1997) *Tales from Ovid*. London: Faber and Faber.

Hume, David (1975) *Enquiries Concerning Human Understanding and Concerning the Principles of Morals*, ed. L.A. Selby Bigge, revised P.H. Nidditch. Oxford: Oxford University Press.

Hume, David (1990) *Dialogues Concerning Natural Religion*, ed. Martin Bell. Harmondsworth: Penguin.

Hursthouse, Rosalind (1987) *Beginning Lives*. Oxford: Blackwell.

Huxley, Aldous (1994) *Brave New World*. London: HarperCollins.

Kafka, Franz (1972) *Metamorphosis and Other Stories*, trans. Willa and Edwin Muir. Harmondsworth: Penguin.

Kamm, F.M. (1992) *Morality, Mortality*. Oxford: Oxford University Press.

Kant, Immanuel (1983) *Perpetual Peace and Other Essays*. Indianapolis: Hackett.

Klemke, E.D. (ed.) (2000) *The Meaning of Life*. Oxford: Oxford University Press.

Kripke, Saul (1980) *Naming and Necessity*. Cambridge, MA: Harvard University Press.

Kureishi, Hanif (2002) *The Body*. London: Faber.

Larkin, Philip (1988) *Collected Poems*. London: Faber and Faber.

Laslett, Peter and Fishkin, James (eds) (1992) *Justice Between Age Groups and Generations*. New Haven, CT: Yale University Press.

Lawrence, Matt (2004) *Lila a Splinter in your Mind: The Philosophy behind the Matrix Trilogy*. Oxford: Blackwell.

Lewis, Hwyel D. (1993) *The Self and Immortality*. London: Macmillan.

Locke, John (1975) *An Essay Concerning Human Understanding*, ed. Peter H. Nidditch. Oxford: Oxford University Press.

Lucretius (1997) *De Rerum Natura*, trans. Sir Ronald Melville. Oxford: Oxford University Press.

Mackie, John (1982) *The Miracle of Theism*. Oxford: The Clarendon Press.

McMahan, Jeff (2002) *The Ethics of Killing*. Oxford: Oxford University Press.

Metz, Thaddeus (2002) 'Recent work on the meaning of life', *Ethics* 112.

Monk, Ray (1990) *Ludwig Wittgenstein: The Duty of Genius*. Harmondsworth: Penguin.

Montaigne, Michel (1965) *Complete Essays*, trans. Donald M. Frame. Stanford, CA: Stanford University Press.

Nagel, Thomas (1979) *Mortal Questions*. Cambridge: Cambridge University Press.

Nagel, Thomas (1986) *The View from Nowhere*. Oxford: Oxford University Press.

Nagel, Thomas (1987) *What Does it All Mean?* Oxford: Oxford University Press.

Noonan, Harold (1991) *Personal Identity*. London: Routledge.

Nozick, Robert (1974) *Anarchy, State and Utopia*. Oxford: Blackwell.

Nozick, Robert (1981) *Philosophical Explanations*. Cambridge, MA: Harvard University Press.

Parfit, Derek (1984) *Reasons and Persons*. Oxford: The Clarendon Press.

Partridge, Ernest (ed.) (1981) *Responsibilities to Future Generations*. Buffalo, NY: Prometheus.

Perry, John (1975) *Personal Identity*. Berkeley, CA: University of California Press.

Plato (1981) *Five Dialogues*, trans. G.M.A. Grube. Indianapolis: Hackett.

Rachels, Stuart (1998) 'Is it good to make happy people?' *Bioethics* 12, 2.

Robinson, John (1963) *Honest to God*. London: SCM.

Rorty, Amélie Oksenberg (1976) (ed.) *The Identities of Persons*. Berkeley, CA: University of California Press.

Runzo, Joseph and Martin, Nancy (eds) (2000) *The Meaning of Life in the World Religions*. Oxford: Oneworld Publications.

Sartre, Jean-Paul (1965) *Nausea*, trans. Robert Baldick. Harmondsworth: Penguin.

Savulescu, Julian (2001) 'Why we should select the best children', *Bioethics* 15, 5/6.

Schopenhauer, Arthur (1970) *Essays and Aphorisms*, trans. R.J. Hollingdale. Harmondsworth: Penguin.

Schweitzer, Albert (1961) *Civilization and Ethics*. London: Allen and Unwin.

Shaw, George Bernard (1974) *Man and Superman*. London: Constable.

Shoemaker, Sydney (1963) *Self-Knowledge and Self-Identity*. Ithaca, NY: Cornell University Press.

Singer, Peter (1993) *Practical Ethics*. Cambridge: Cambridge University Press.

Singer, Peter (1994) *Rethinking Life and Death*. Oxford: Oxford University Press.

Smart, J.J.C. and Haldane, J.J. (1996) *Atheism and Theism*. Oxford: Blackwell.

Smart, J.J.C. and Williams, Bernard (1973) *Utilitarianism, For and Against*. Cambridge: Cambridge University Press.

Swift, Jonathan (1986) *Gulliver's Travels*. Oxford: Oxford University Press.

Swinburne, Richard (1996) *Is There a God?* Oxford: Oxford University Press.

Unger, Peter (1990) *Identity, Consciousness and Value*. Oxford: Oxford University Press.

Voltaire (1974) *Candide*, trans. John Butt. Harmondsworth: Penguin.

Warburton, Nigel (1992) *Philosophy: The Basics*. London: Routledge.

Williams, Bernard (1973) *Problems of the Self*. Cambridge: Cambridge University Press.

Wittgenstein, Ludwig (1974) *Tractatus Logico-Philosophicus*, trans. D.F. Pears and B.F. McGuinness. London: Routledge and Kegan Paul.

Wolf, Susan (1997) 'Happiness and meaning: two aspects of the good life', in *Social Philosophy and Policy* 14, 1.

Wollstonecraft, Mary (1788) *Original Stories from Real Life*. London: J. Johnson.

Name Index

I include here the names of all people, real and fictional, occurring in the main text.

Subject Index

I include here all the major and many of the minor subjects and themes dealt with or referred to in the main text.